J.C. LEYENDECKER

J.C. LEYENDECKER
BY MICHAEL SCHAU

WATSON-GUPTILL PUBLICATIONS/NEW YORK

Copyright © 1974 by Watson-Guptill Publications
First published 1974 in New York by Watson-Guptill Publications,
a division of Billboard Publications, Inc.,
One Astor Plaza, New York, N.Y. 10036

All rights reserved. No part of this publication
may be reproduced or used in any form or by any means—graphic,
electronic, or mechanical, including photocopying, recording, taping,
or information storage and retrieval systems—without
written permission of the publisher.

Manufactured in the U.S.A.

Library of Congress Cataloging in Publication Data
Schau, Michael, 1945–
  J. C. Leyendecker,
    1. Leyendecker, J   C   1874–1951.
I. Leyendecker, J.C., 1874–1951.
NC975.5.L4S32   741.9'73   74–7125
ISBN 0-8230-2757-0

First Printing, 1974

For Carole

CONTENTS

ACKNOWLEDGMENTS	9
LIST OF COLOR PLATES	10
INTRODUCTION	13
CHRONOLOGY	47
ILLUSTRATIONS	49
POSTERS	63
ADVERTISEMENTS	81
MAGAZINE COVERS	127
CONCLUSION	204
INDEX	205

ACKNOWLEDGMENTS

Even though J.C. Leyendecker was one of America's most popular illustrators during the first half of this century, there are only a few bits of written information about the man's life and position in the history of American illustration. Assembling even a modest biography and a collection of Leyendecker's pictures for this book was made possible through the generosity and interest of many, many people. My role in relation to their large part in this project is best described by Montaigne's words: "I gather the flowers by the wayside, by the brooks and in the meadows, and only the string with which I bind them together is my own."

Among individuals who opened their collections, searched their memories, and assisted in finding data were Bela Bordas, Stephen R. Sanderson, Pierce Rice, Alex Chasky, Remsen Duryea, Ernest T. Thompson, Sr., Frank Liljegren, Fred Dueren, George C. Adams, Edmond Fitzgerald, Pete Martin, William H. White, Sr., John Spiers, Neil Hamilton, Herbert S. Stone, Jr., Ial Radom, Larry Kritcher, and Martin Ullman.

Special gratitude is expressed to Mrs. James F. Parr (Peggy Sullivan) and other members of the Sullivan family, cousins of the Leyendeckers.

Several companies—many for which Leyendecker created advertising art—graciously cooperated, including Curtis Publishing Company, Cluett, Peabody & Co., Inc. (with special thanks to Robert Clark), Hart Schaffner & Marx, Interwoven Socks, Inc., Procter & Gamble, and The Timken Company.

I wish also to thank the Columbia University Library, the Metropolitan Museum of Art of New York, the Art Institute of Chicago, the Chicago Historical Society, the Boston Public Library, the New Rochelle Public Library, the New York City Public Library, the Museum of the City of New York, and the Berry-Hill Galleries of New York.

Donald Holden at Watson-Guptill worked zealously to make the Leyendecker book idea a reality, and editor Susan Davis, whose middle name surely must be "Patience," made many knowledgable suggestions. Her work, in matters of both text and pictures, has proven invaluable to the project.

Most importantly I owe a large debt of gratitude to Jane and Stephen Klain. Not only did Jane introduce me to Leyendecker's pictures, but the Klains have shared their art, research, and enthusiasm when it was most needed. In truth, the book would have been much more difficult, if not impossible, without their generous assistance.

COLOR PLATES

Posters

	Page
Poster for *One Fair Daughter*, May 1895	65
The Century magazine's Midsummer Holiday Number, August 1896	66
The Inland Printer magazine, October 1897	67
The Chap-Book magazine, 1899	68
Up To Date magazine, 1899	69
Up To Date magazine, 1899	70
Up To Date magazine, 1899	71
Success magazine's Christmas Number, 1900	72
"Rowing," *Scribner's* magazine, 1906	73
Poster for University of Pennsylvania, 1906	74
"Weapons for Liberty," 1917	75
"Order Coal Now," 1917	76
U.S. Navy Recruitment, 1918	77
"Enlist Today, U.S. Marines," 1918	78
General MacArthur, 1944	79
General Eisenhower, 1944	80

Advertisements

Ivory Soap, 1900	97
Rogers & Company, 1900	98
Kellogg's Corn Flakes, 1917	99
Arrow Collar, 1910	100–101
Arrow Collar, 1913	102
Arrow Collar	103
Arrow Collar	104–105
Arrow Collar, ca. 1922	106
B. Kuppenheimer & Company	107
Arrow Collar, 1912	108–109
Arrow Collar	110
Arrow Collar	110
Arrow Collar	110
Arrow Collar	110
Arrow Collar, 1929	111
B. Kuppenheimer & Company	112

Magazine Covers | *Page*

The Inland Printer, December 1897	129
Success magazine, April 1903	130
Success magazine, June 1904	131
Success magazine, December 1905	132
"When Shall We Fly?" *Collier's,* February 23, 1907	133
"Westward Ho!" *Collier's,* December 7, 1907	134
Success Magazine, February 1908	135
The Popular Magazine, March 1909	136
"College Football," *The Century Illustrated Monthly Magazine,* November 1909	137
The Saturday Evening Post, April 3, 1926	138
The Saturday Evening Post, November 26, 1927	139
The Saturday Evening Post, January 1, 1927	140
The Saturday Evening Post, June 2, 1928	141
The Saturday Evening Post, November 24, 1928	142
The Saturday Evening Post, June 29, 1929	143
The Saturday Evening Post, June 8, 1929	144
The Saturday Evening Post, July 4, 1931	145
The Saturday Evening Post, July 4, 1932	146
The Saturday Evening Post, August 6, 1932	147
The Saturday Evening Post, December 31, 1932	148
The Saturday Evening Post, December 23, 1933	149
The Saturday Evening Post, March 31, 1934	150
The Saturday Evening Post, July 7, 1934	151
The Saturday Evening Post, September 15, 1934	152
The Saturday Evening Post, December 29, 1934	153
The Saturday Evening Post, February 23, 1935	154
The Saturday Evening Post, October 19, 1935	155
The Saturday Evening Post, February 15, 1936	156
The Saturday Evening Post, April 11, 1936	157
The Saturday Evening Post, March 27, 1937	158
The Saturday Evening Post, January 20, 1940	159
The American Weekly magazine, November 24, 1946	160

The Leyendecker brothers, Frank (left) and Joe, in their rooms in Paris, 1896.

INTRODUCTION

As America begins to rediscover the rich heritage of its decorative and commercial artists and illustrators, the art of J.C. Leyendecker is again emerging. Leyendecker developed as a major graphic arts talent around the turn of the century and proceeded to become America's most popular illustrator. His fine reputation—the product of hundreds of pictures and several decades—had already begun to fade in the late forties, during the last years of his life, but with the revived interest in the work of the great illustrators, Leyendecker's brilliance is receiving renewed recognition.

Little is known about the details of Leyendecker's personal life. He guarded his privacy, would not indulge in publicity, and left no decorative public works that could become monuments to his large talent. Certainly no significant works of criticism exist on his art. Not even chatty, little intimate anecdotes—so readily available in books by and about other illustrators of the period—are known in Leyendecker's case. It would have been illuminating to have them, but the lack of such material is itself a key to Leyendecker's personality.

The sensibility, style, and technique of the man must be found in his pictures —in the posters, illustrations, advertisements, and hundreds of magazine covers. Verbal confirmation of Leyendecker's sensitivity, elegance, vitality, and pride of craftsmanship is not necessary; the pictures say it all.

Joseph Christian Leyendecker was born March 23, 1874, at Montabour in southwest Germany, a tiny village on the Rhine. The local Catholic Church is the only source of the town's historical information, and the parish office has this official record of the birth: "C.J. (*sic*) Leyendecker, baptized March 29, 1874, Son of Peter Leyendecker (Catholic), a coachman from Dernbach, and Elizabeth Ortseifen (Catholic), married in Montabour. Godparents Christian Joseph Leyendecker and Mathilde Goldhausen, both of Dernbach."

The parish marriage book offers what little background is available on Leyendecker's parents: "Peter Leyendecker, born September 16, 1838, at Dernbach; parents Peter Leyendecker and Anna Maria Görg, married couple of Dernbach. Married May, 1869, to Elizabeth Ortseifen, born September 29, 1845, at Wirzenborn; parents Christian Ortseifen and Anna Roth, married."

Joseph was the first-born son; his brother Frank Xavier was born three years later. A sister, Augusta, the third and last child, arrived after the family had emigrated to America.

Peter Leyendecker brought his family to Chicago in 1882. It is believed that the four came under the auspices of Elizabeth's uncle, a well-to-do brewer who served in minor Chicago government posts and who had emigrated several years earlier. Peter Leyendecker settled his family on South Park Avenue and went to work at his uncle-in-law's McAvoy Brewery.

The only reliable account of Joe's childhood is a modest, 300-word profile written by him in 1938 for *The Saturday Evening Post*:

"The Leyendeckers are of Dutch ancestry, though we came to America in 1882 from Montabour. I was eight at the time and was already covering school books with rudely colored examples of my work. At home I kept myself busy with more pretentious paintings which, for want of canvas, were done on oilcloth of the common kitchen variety. Whatever their faults, these pictures lacked nothing in size. They were all dutifully presented to long-suffering friends and relatives."

Whether or not Joe graduated from high school is not known, but at the age of 16 he decided to devote his full time to an art career. For a lower-middle-class family like the Leyendeckers in 1889, formal art study for their sons was a luxury that could not be afforded. However, Joe's parents recognized in his work a promise that deserved development, and it is to their credit that they saved what funds they could to assist him later. Frank, who also exhibited considerable drawing talent, but was "the second son," did not receive the same consideration.

Joe did the only thing possible for a boy in his circumstances—he apprenticed at a Chicago engraving house, J. Manz & Company on Monroe Street. "When I was sixteen, I felt I'd reached the saturation point in the oilcloth field," Leyendecker continued in his piece for *The Saturday Evening Post*. "So I decided to find a job and gain some practical experience in the profession of being an artist. I still remember boarding an open cable car one windy day with three large canvases wrapped in newspaper and fighting my way through the crowded streets to an engraving house where I showed my samples. The boss inspected a stag at bay, a chariot race and a Bibical subject, with amusement, but he did tell me to report for work. I now had a job—that is, I was an apprentice without pay—with a chance to learn the art business in the intervals between running errands. The new half-tone process was not used in our shop until a year later. In the meantime, I'd become a salaried man, starting at two dollars a week. I could now attend Vanderpoel's class at the Art Institute three nights a week."

Leyendecker was enrolled in the evening drawing class at the Art Institute for the winter term of 1889–90. During the next five years he took a variety of courses, studying mainly with John H. Vanderpoel, who had been a pupil of Boulanger and Lefebvre at the Académie Julian in Paris, where the Leyendecker brothers would eventually study. Throughout his career, Joe stressed the importance of Vanderpoel's guidance in helping to develop his talent as a draftsman.

While Joe had a natural gift for drawing, the Art Institute classes helped shape his technique and taught him refinement and control. This won Joe a promotion at Manz from part-time artist/errand boy to full illustrator, giving him a salary increase and the opportunity to attend some Art Institute day classes as well.

For the school term 1892–93 he took an "antiques class" with Vanderpoel and Miss Enella Benedict, also a Julian graduate and student of Lefebvre, Constant, and Laurens. The course as described in the 1892 catalog included "heads

An 1895 advertisement by Leyendecker for J. Manz & Company, the Chicago engraving house to which he apprenticed in 1889. Courtesy Chicago Historical Society.

and figures from cast in full light and shade; still life in colors, modeling and designing recommended; students in the class are often permitted to make studies from life." Frank Leyendecker, then 15, took the evening "antiques" course that same term. Frank had foregone education beyond the elementary level to apprentice, at 13, to Carl Brandt, a stained-glass worker originally from Vienna.

At the Manz company Leyendecker created art for many advertisements, including house ads for Manz, and posters for new novels such as the popular *Dolly Dialogues* by Anthony Hope Hawkins. In 1893, when he was 19, he began a set of illustrations for an edition of *The Bible* that was printed by Manz in 1894. A monumental work, it consisted of some sixty pictures that illustrated traditional views of well-known Testament stories (page 51). There is little of the crisp, precise stroke that was Leyendecker's trademark in later years, but the scenes are drawn on a bold, grand scale and are remarkable when you consider the age of the artist.

That year Leyendecker took both day and evening courses with Vanderpoel in a "life class" detailed in the catalog as "costumed and nude life; composition." Frank enrolled in the same course in the evening, and the following term the two took an advanced evening "life class" together.

"There followed two years at the Académie Julian with Jean-Paul Laurens and Benjamin Constant, two famous artists of the period, as instructors," wrote Leyendecker in his autobiographical sketch. This one sentence is a deceptively abrupt summation of the two years that were so personally exciting for the young artist—so decidedly important to the formation of the unique Leyendecker style.

The Leyendecker family had saved to send Joe to Paris for art study, and managed to send Frank with him. With his position at Manz, Joe too was able to put money aside for the trip. One story has it that Joe's cash prize from an art contest gave him the freedom to leave Chicago and spend two years abroad; this is not quite the circumstance.

The competition referred to was *The Century* magazine poster contest, announced early in 1896; the winning cover was to appear on the August Midsummer Holiday issue (page 66). Joe submitted a cover design, a woman's head in green, red, and gold in the art nouveau style. A panel of judges, including artist Elihu Vedder, F. Hopkinson Smith, and Henry Hardenburgh, selected Leyendecker's poster the winner. Maxfield Parrish, already well-established in the field, won second prize.

The acclaim for his entry was a great honor for Joe and the small cash prize was no doubt helpful, but it certainly was not enough to support two young men for two years in Paris.

Frank, now 18, was sent with Joe not only to study but also to provide companionship. The two took courses together, shared rooms, and toured the city, its salons and galleries. They were extremely close in these early years. Joe was then —and he remained—a very shy man who preferred expression through pictures. Frank was also quiet and sensitive, but less obviously so than Joe.

J.C. Leyendecker was a handsome young man, a bit shorter than average. He had no noticeable accent although he knew no English until he was eight. He had a slight stutter, but only at times, as his friends remember. Artist Norman Rockwell, a friend of the brothers for many years, describes them in his autobiography, *My Adventures as an Illustrator* (Doubleday & Company, 1960). To Rockwell, Joe and Frank were "both very handsome—dark complexioned with high cheekbones and straight delicately molded noses, like Spaniards. And trim, well built, the line of their jackets falling straight from shoulder to hip."

Joe and Frank must have been overwhelmed by their first sight of 1896 Paris. Not only had they so long saved for and so eagerly awaited study there, but the architectural splendor, gaiety, and sophistication of the city must have been more to their taste than the comparative roughness of Chicago.

Paris was a vast open-air museum in which many of its most interesting artists were represented; the city was covered bank to bank with flamboyantly colorful art nouveau posters. The designs of Cherêt, the most popular poster artist of the time, were everywhere, as were Mucha's graceful ads for cigarette papers and Bernhardt plays and Lautrec's ads for bicycles and the Moulin Rouge.

The Leyendecker brothers were influenced by that popular art which surrounded them as they walked the boulevards, and on many occasions they used the lines and colors of art nouveau. Yet they were enrolled at the prestigious Académie Julian where the new styles were contemptuously labeled "fads" and from which then-current art was excluded. Such innovations could not be acknowledged, much less tolerated; and the newer art remained where it was seen—in the streets. The Julian, under the guidance of Adolphe William Bouguereau (1825–1905), taught the prevailing tastes of the French art establishment. Study of the classics was considered the only worthy endeavor, and excellence in making exact copies the goal instilled in students.

Several terms earlier Alphonse Mucha had studied at the Julian, as had Bonnard and Maurice Prendergast. Marcel Duchamp entered the Académie but soon dropped out, frustrated at what he considered the too-traditional approach to art. Henri Matisse, who enrolled for the 1892–93 semester, could bear only a few weeks of such required classes as copying plaster casts before he quickly departed.

The Julian atmosphere was evidently not disagreeable to the Leyendeckers. Joe had come to Paris to extend the art education he had begun in Chicago. Already a superb draftsman, he must have felt the Julian could sharpen his talent

One of many sketches done by J.C. in Paris, 1897. Collection of the author.

and give him additional background in technique. Although a popular pastime among Paris art students of the day was collecting commercial posters, pried with damp sponges from walls, fences, and billboards during nighttime raids, photographs show no such posters or prints in the Leyendeckers' Paris rooms. In fact the brothers had a distinct preference for works acceptable at the Julian.

The lessons learned at the Julian and at the Colarossi, where the brothers took additional classes, remained with Leyendecker throughout his life. Years later as a teacher at Pickett Institute in New York, he would strictly employ the same procedures. One of his students there recalls Leyendecker's reaction to attempts at innovations during a copying session: "There is plenty of time for that later, but for now, do not try to improve upon the masters."

Adolphe Bouguereau was one of the most famous salon painters in France during the last decades of the 19th century. His influence was enormous. Yet to those who disagreed with his school and its precepts, Bouguereau was an egomaniacal schoolmaster who enjoyed having young artists copy his style.

Leyendecker showed immediate promise and was given special attention by the Julian's most important artists-teachers, Benjamin Constant (1845–1902) and Jean-Paul Laurens (1838–1921). Constant was famous for painting Near East and mythological subjects, a taste which the Leyendeckers, especially Frank, acquired as well. Constant's great murals and ceilings in glorification of French history, Ste. Genevieve, Beethoven, Colbert, and the like, won him a wide following, more commissions than he could accept, and the Legion of Honor in 1878. Throughout Leyendecker's life, he cherished his two years with Constant and Laurens and gave them much credit for his own success.

Joe was considered one of the most talented young men to attend the Julian for many years before or after his terms there. Fellow classmates, mainly American and English men—all older than the brothers if we can judge by the class picture—recall that the monthly prize given by Bouguereau for the best work by a student invariably went to Joe. The few times it did not, it was won by Frank. Joe's achievements at the Académie were so highly regarded that several of his classroom drawings, including a memorable life-size nude, were displayed in the school's permanent exhibition, where they remained until a World War II bombing raid destroyed them.

The Académie Julian class of Benjamin Constant (front row), Paris, 1896. Frank is standing in the back row and Joe is standing in the second row.

During his two years in Paris, Leyendecker's most notable public success was a one-man exhibition at the Salon Champs du Mars in April 1897. The works displayed were very much in keeping with the type of painting taught at the Julian. Included in the small showing were a number of portraits and various sketches done around Paris (the brothers' hours away from the classroom were often spent sketching and painting the city and its people). A charcoal study of Frank served as the show's catalog coverpiece.

Just as important as the study of art to Leyendecker's future career was the knowledge—reinforced by the popular art all over Paris—that there was no stigma attached to being a commercial artist. Although America crowned industry its king during the period, and many talented artists were royally rewarded for promoting business through commercial art, Paris was where Leyendecker found that commercial art could also carry with it prestige. In 1889, for example, Cherêt received the Legion of Honor for "creating a new branch of art by applying art to commercial and industrial paintings." There were money and fame to be won, Leyendecker could see, by painting for the masses in the streets as well as for the few in the museums.

This charcoal portrait of Frank Leyendecker was among the works shown in Joe's one-man exhibition in Paris, 1897. The picture was also used as the cover for the exhibition's catalog.

The notoriety of winning *The Century* poster contest in 1896 gave Joe the opportunity to begin his professional career even before he left the Julian and Paris. He did the January 1897 cover for the famous *Inland Printer* published in Chicago. The editor was so pleased with the work that he asked Joe to submit more covers from Paris, and then more. By the end of 1897 Joe had created all the cover designs for *The Inland Printer*'s twelve issues that year (page 161), and in the next two years he did additional cover paintings.

The dozen covers completed in 1897 reveal what a strong influence Paris and currently popular French art had on him. Individual though the pictures are, they heavily reflect the popular French styles—and they have elegance and maturity not evident in earlier works.

Joe and Frank sailed for America in August 1897, and in September they opened a studio together in Chicago's Stock Exchange Building. Joe was 23, Frank 20, and they had no problem finding commercial art assignments. Joe continued to do some work on a free-lance basis for Manz & Company, as well as ads for Carson Pirie & Scott department store, A.B. Kirschbaum Clothiers, and McAvoy Brewery.

Leyendecker's poster for the popular *Chap-Book* was published in October 1897. His design, "Woman with Cat" (page 68), was the sixteenth and final poster issued by Stone & Kimball and Herbert S. Stone Company to advertise *Chap-Book*. It followed Toulouse-Lautrec's *Chap-Book* poster, and considering that earlier works for the publication had been done by Will H. Bradley, Frank Hazenplug, Claude Bragdon, and Elisha Bird, Joe was in prestigious company.

Additional recognition came in January 1898. The brothers' studio had been open three months when Joe's twelve *Inland Printer* covers and posters, the last of which had just been published the month before, were put on exhibition. A comment in the March 1898 *Inland Printer* noted: "An exhibition of the 12 original *Inland Printer* poster drawings of Mr. J.C. Leyendecker was opened at the Kimball Cafetier, Chicago, on January 11, the 'cozy corner' of this popular cafe, with its well-arranged lighting, being a nook well-suited to the proper showing of the work of this talented artist."

Although they shared the studio and Frank was hired almost as often as his brother for various jobs, Frank also pursued his interest in designing and making stained-glass windows. From the start the studio was a success and the Leyendeckers' work much in demand. The brothers remained close, but their differences in goals and work habits became clearly established in these first months at the new studio. Only later would these differences become conflicts.

Frank did not have his older brother's enthusiasm for doing only commercial art. He hoped eventually to turn to the fine arts, or so he often said. Yet he produced little work of this type. Whether or not he lacked the vision or self-confidence to attempt such work is hard to tell. But it is possible to understand the difficulties Frank experienced throughout his life: he was "the other Leyendecker." His direction was set by the public, art critics, and editors. Even within the Leyendecker family it was Joe who was urged to push, to excel. It didn't matter that some thought Frank as good as Joe—and some even better.

Frank was probably also urged to continue commercial work by Joe, who believed a successful artist was a fine draftsman, had flair for color, was exacting about detail—and rich. Joe worked hard until his death because of his firm belief that an artist should spend beyond his current earning power. "If you spend more than you have at the moment, you will force yourself to work" was his advice to young artists over the years.

This is not to say that Joe would do slapdash work to satisfy an editor or agency; quite the opposite was true. He could ignore deadlines, even deliver wet canvases, if it meant turning in the finest work possible.

Frank hadn't the same determination to reach the top of the graphic arts field. He accepted commissions for magazine covers, ads, posters, but—especially in later years—he would delay, sometimes until the job had to be offered to another artist. However, as a young man forging a career, he worked enthusiastically. For the time being, he was enjoying the new success of the shared studio as much as Joe.

In 1899, Joe was hired by companies that gave his work national exposure. The wider audience and larger fees more than anything helped the brothers decide to leave Chicago and move to New York City where better jobs, remuneration, and fame were to be had for the talented illustrator.

That year Stone & Kimball published *Spanish Peggy,* a novel by Mary Hartwell Catherwood, illustrated in part by Joe and with the cover designed by him. Toward the end of the year, he created an advertisement for the Procter & Gamble Company for Ivory soap (page 97). The ad, which ran in magazines the following year, was beautifully designed as a mosaic, executed in oil, and printed in full color. Whether or not the ad greatly assisted the sales of Ivory soap is not known, but the picture itself was so popular and much-requested by the public that Procter & Gamble offered it in reprints—for two Ivory soap wrappers.

The most significant step forward for Leyendecker came when his first cover illustration for *The Saturday Evening Post* was accepted in 1899. The drawing, printed in black and white (page 26), illustrated a story on the Spanish-American war, which had erupted the previous year. Leyendecker remembered: "My first *Post* cover appeared May 20, 1899. There was nothing distinctive in the appearance of the first few numbers; it was not until George Horace Lorimer became editor that color was introduced and the cover became a design complete in itself."

True, this initial cover, compared with the 321 others by J.C. Leyendecker that appeared on *The Saturday Evening Post* during the next four decades, was not especially distinguished—but it was the first. Though the artist did not do a second *Post* cover until 1903, this initial piece established a relationship with the magazine and gave him additional national exposure.

At the height of his popularity Leyendecker produced more than a dozen *Post* covers a year, and was paid $1,500 per cover. Conflicting accounts say the fee was $2,000 for each cover, but no written contract ever existed between Leyendecker and *The Post*. Although the general procedure for selling a *Post* cover illustration was to submit a finished picture to Lorimer for approval, Leyendecker was the only *Post* artist (with the later exception of Norman Rockwell) who was permitted to submit a sketch for approval, and then given the go-ahead based on it.

As *The Post*'s most important cover artist for decades, Leyendecker painted all the front pieces for the holiday numbers, as well as many in between. His Easter, Independence Day, Thanksgiving, and Christmas covers were annual events for the readers who numbered in the millions. And he created the annual New Year baby that for almost forty years was the symbol of the New Year for *The Post*. The first cherub (which over the years evolved into the more familiar New Year baby) appeared in 1906, and became as much a symbol of that holiday as Santa Claus is of Christmas. Through the years, *The Post* New Year babies chronicled what was foremost on the collective American mind that year: women's suffrage (December 30, 1911, page 176); Prohibition (January 3, 1920, page 186); hope for economic upswing during the Depression (December 31, 1932, page 148); and

(Left) Leyendecker's first cover for The Saturday Evening Post, May 20, 1899. Courtesy William H. White, Sr. (Right) The first New Year cherub done by Leyendecker for The Saturday Evening Post, December 29, 1906. The baby became a Post New Year tradition, and a Leyendecker design was on the cover of the magazine's first issue every year thereafter until 1943. This 1906 cherub is recording New Year's resolutions, including one signed "J.C. Leyendecker." Courtesy Curtis Publishing Company.

(Left) Actor Neil Hamilton, a friend of Leyendecker's for over thirty years, posed as the doughboy for this Thanksgiving Post cover, 1918. (Right) Earl Williams (left) and Howard Davenport, Jr., posed for this Independence Day cover for The Saturday Evening Post, 1937. Courtesy Curtis Publishing Company.

victory over Nazi Germany (January 2, 1943, which was also Leyendecker's last *Post* cover, page 201).

The term *"Saturday Evening Post* artist" has often been a label of scorn—and justified in some cases. But Leyendecker managed the necessary wide appeal in his pictures without aiming at the lowest common denominator. Although in some circles *The Post* was considered a "magazine for farmers," Leyendecker consistently exposed the readership to a sophistication of design and subject that covered such diverse areas as Egyptian art motifs, mythological beings, and American patriots modeled after Bernini statues. He could be appropriately sentimental, but also clever and stylish when it was expected.

This immediate, wide exposure of his work through *The Post* was agreeable to Leyendecker, but there were, of course, disadvantages as well as advantages to being a *Post* cover artist. The impermanence of the work was the most severe drawback. One week a picture was before the admiring eyes of millions of Americans; the next week it was thrown out with the old magazines—the original kept in a closet at the artist's home.

Throughout his life J.C. refused commissions that would have given his work a permanent audience. He was asked to do murals for the Boston Public Library, the ceiling of the main reading room at the New York City Public Library, and many similar decorative works. He declined them all. It is regrettable for us that Leyendecker so exclusively pursued one aspect of art rather than lending his talent to other fields. His fine illustrations strongly suggest what major decorative pictures might have been his legacy, had he only attempted them.

Early in 1900, the Leyendeckers closed their Chicago studio and moved East. There is some evidence that they first stopped in Philadelphia for a short time, and perhaps considered working there, but they opened a studio in New York City at 7 East 32nd Street that same year. The first decade of the new century proved one of the most productive and varied of Joe's career. He worked constantly, creating some of the finest pictures he would do, and established himself with magazines and companies that would use his pictures for decades to follow.

Joe illustrated parts of "The Rubaiyat of Omar Khayyam" in 1901 for *Delineator Magazine*. The format of a set of pictures, a frontispiece followed by six illustrations and back plate with the text fully integrated into the overall design, was highly successful for the magazine, and prompted other magazines to commission similar illustrations by him. Between 1901 and 1910 he illustrated "The Radiant Christ," "Love Songs from the Wagner Operas" (pages 52–53), "A Song of Faith" (pages 58–59), "The Great Guest Comes" (page 55), "Centuries Ago," and "The Swarming of the White Bees" for such magazines as *Delineator, Century,* and *Scribner's.* These works comprise some of Leyendecker's most imaginative efforts.

That Leyendecker's most varied work was done during these first years in New York says less about the artist and his ambition and ability than about the circumstances in which he and all illustrators of the era found themselves. The Golden Age of Illustration was definitely on the wane. The day when books and periodicals depended upon artists to illuminate the text was all but gone. More than any other factor, the process of photoengraving put artists and other craftsmen in the background as photographs proved less expensive and had a wider appeal. Fine artists who had made careers as book and magazine illustrators were soon able only to find work painting pictures to accompany advertising copy. Fortunately for his survival in the art field, Joe began his career late enough in the era so that he could adapt. He was as comfortable illustrating Egerton R. Williams' novel of knighthood, *Ridolfo, the Coming of the Dawn* (page 56), as he was creating a memorable image that would sell menswear. He was successful because he could execute any illustration with both style and conviction.

In 1905, Leyendecker received what became his most important commercial art assignment. He was hired to do advertisements by Cluett, Peabody & Co., Inc., manufacturers of Arrow brand detachable shirt collars. Many of his *Post* and *Collier's* magazine covers had featured handsome, smartly dressed young men; these more than hinted at the artist's ability to create a dashing image for the product. Yet it was bigger than that. Over the next twenty-five years, the "Arrow Collar Man" became the symbol of fashionable American manhood. As surely as Charles Dana Gibson created a prototype of the elegant young woman, Leyendecker, through the Arrow ads, defined the ideal of the American male: a dignified, clear-eyed man of taste, manners, and quality.

Over the years, the image projected by the Arrow Man ads boosted the sales of at least 400 styles of shirt collars. Such future screen stars as Fredric March, Brian Donlevy, and Jack Mulhall were models. Today, it is difficult to imagine the

A portrait of novelist-playwright Rex E. Beach (1877–1949) by J.C. Leyendecker. The easel picture, one of the few Leyendecker ever did, is inscribed in the lower right-hand corner: "to my friend Rex Beach, a souvenir of our trip down the Santee, J.C. Leyendecker, '12." (Rex Beach was no relation to Leyendecker's friend Charles Beach.) Courtesy Berry-Hill Galleries, New York City.

sensation created by Leyendecker's pictures. But fan mail for one model or another arrived at Cluett, Peabody by the ton, and in one month in the early 1920s the Arrow Man received 17,000 fan letters, gifts, marriage proposals, and notes threatening suicide—a deluge surpassing even Rudolph Valentino's mail at the star's apex. The term "Arrow Collar Man" became a common epithet for any handsome, nattily dressed gent, and the Arrow Man was the subject of admiring poems, songs, and even a Broadway play. In 1918 Arrow Collar sales rose to over $32 million. But World War I taught soldiers the practicality and comfort of attached collars, and detachables began to fall from favor thereafter. Yet Leyendecker continued to paint Arrow men for the new line of shirts.

The first model whom Leyendecker used for the Arrow Collar ads was Charles Beach, a strikingly handsome man and a model of Joe's since 1901. Beach's background is a mystery, nor do we know definitely how he and Joe met or at what exact point their relationship began. It is known that, with time, Beach came to be Joe's closest companion, assistant, and business manager. The details of their association—one that would last for almost fifty years—are shrouded in the solitary life they built and are the cause of curious speculation even today. But Beach's relationship with the artist, one so total as to eventually exclude Frank, deserves more than passing mention.

In *My Adventures as an Illustrator,* Norman Rockwell recalls Beach as "tall, powerfully-built and extraordinarily handsome.... He spoke with a clipped British accent and was always beautifully dressed. His manners were polished and impeccable." Since Rockwell was a close friend of the Leyendeckers and since almost no other person has written about Leyendecker or his work, no matter how brief, those who today remember anything about Leyendecker's personal life remember him through Rockwell's book.

As a young man, Rockwell idolized Leyendecker and his work. Joe, E.A. Abbey, and Howard Pyle were his ideals. Once Rockwell confided to a model, who had also worked for Leyendecker, that as a teenager in New Rochelle, New York, where the Leyendeckers later lived, Rockwell would take every opportunity just to catch a glimpse of Joe. Rockwell admitted that he would go to the town railroad station in the evening hopeful of seeing Joe step off the commuter train from New York and into his chauffeured limousine.

The Arrow Collar Man. An advertisement for the Concord-style collar, 1910. Charles Beach was probably the model.

Rockwell records that he greatly admired Leyendecker, studied his work, and later sought his friendship. He describes Joe as a robust, charming man—until Charles Beach arrived on the scene, managed some perverse hold on the artist, insinuated himself into Leyendecker's home and career, and little by little took over the artist's life. Eventually, according to Rockwell, Beach maliciously caused a rift between Joe and Frank that forced Frank, and their sister Augusta, to leave the home they shared. Rockwell believes these circumstances caused Frank to turn to drugs, which led to his early death.

The basics of this account are factual, but Rockwell's interpretation of these facts is open to question, particularly since no other sources confirm most of the details. The memoir must be recognized for what it is—personal and overdramatized in parts.

Beach did become a member of the Leyendecker household. He did become Joe's closest companion and played a very important part in the artist's life during the fifty years they spent together. It is also true that Beach's presence was later a point of contention between Joe and Frank, that Frank left the Leyendecker mansion, and that he died shortly thereafter. But Rockwell's notion that Joe was an outgoing, life-loving man until Beach's malevolence transformed him into a withdrawn, neurotic recluse is inconsistent with reality. Rockwell's insistence that the "hermitlike" Joe spent his life in his mansion on Mt. Tom Road in New Rochelle, never ventured out, saw no one but Rockwell, Beach, and a few family members is contradicted by others. Many people alive today remember visiting Joe at his home or going on excursions with him away from the mansion. Joe was not reclusive, but simply private, a solitary man as many artists are, preoccupied with his art and later with his lavish gardens surrounding the mansion.

Many who knew Beach did not like him. But others, including some Leyendecker family members, thought him pleasant, polite, and good for Joe. Certainly, Rockwell's heated view that Beach "was a real parasite—like some huge, white, cold insect clinging to Joe's back," was an irrational picture, even to those who did not particularly care for Beach.

If nothing else, Beach earned his keep. He hired Joe's models; laid out props, brushes, and other materials each morning; personally delivered finished pictures to agencies and magazine offices; kept records of engagements and correspondence;

did the shopping—in short, took care of the details of daily life, which left Leyendecker free to do his work. True, Beach was excessively protective; it is a fact that he became unusually possessive and eventually got a commission on each piece of work Joe did. Many recall he even began to think of the pictures as a collaboration and would refer to them as "our work."

Rockwell's most uncharitable comment is that Leyendecker "could never paint a woman with any sympathy." This criticism—which sounds more like an indirect attack on Joe's personal life than a description of his work—is contradicted by the many fine female figures in this book.

What Leyendecker's many admirers will find least convincing, however, is Rockwell's deprecation of Leyendecker's talent: "But for days on end he (Joe) wouldn't talk to anyone but Beach and his models. As a result his work suffered. It was perhaps true that there had always been more technique than feeling in it. He didn't look at a picture as the depiction of a scene, a scene with flesh-blood-and-breath people in it; he saw it as a technical problem. Whenever he was tired and discouraged about a picture, he'd just put more technique into it. And technique alone is a pretty hollow thing."

The mass magazine audience is unconcerned with painting techniques, but responds to human warmth and imagination. Joe could never have been popular with millions of Americans for so long if he had nothing to offer but shallow technical prowess. He remained successful because he was a sensitive, aware, feeling man throughout his life.

The overwhelming success, both artistic and commercial, of Joe's Arrow campaign, prompted other producers of men's clothing to seek him out, hopeful the Leyendecker touch could lend elegance to their products as well. Such clothiers as B. Kuppenheimer, Hart Schaffner & Marx, and Interwoven Socks gave him a free hand in presenting their products. If less spectacular than the Arrow pictures, his work for the many other clothing companies comprises some of the most stylish ads of that type ever produced.

The Leyendecker name was becoming well known in America, and the public watched for work with the familiar Leyendecker signatures, both J.C. and F.X. Frank was doing covers for *The Saturday Evening Post, Vanity Fair, Collier's, Life,* and other periodicals, as well as book illustrations and advertisements. In

1907, the brothers moved from 32nd Street to a large, well-staffed house near Washington Square in Greenwich Village, and Joe opened a luxurious studio in the Beaux Arts Building, which still stands at Sixth Avenue and 40th Street, overlooking Bryant Park. Frank preferred to work at home and did not share Joe's studio.

The J.C. Leyendecker style—the very wide, deliberate stroke done with authority and control—was firmly established by this time. It did not take a student of illustration to pick out the distinctive treatment of subject. A Leyendecker picture was, if nothing else, to the point. He seldom overpainted, preferring to interest the viewer with the omissions as well as the parts included.

Leyendecker sketched constantly. Even when not working on a specific picture, he would fill canvases with sketches of anything and everything. Since he refused to use photographs, the volumes of sketches were saved for later reference. He would often paint a model's head for an Arrow ad, leaving the area below the neck blank for the day when a new collar style was needed. Or he would sketch flowers in his garden and store the studies for future use. *Saturday Evening Post* covers were finished months in advance of publication. The annual Leyendecker Easter cover, for example, which invariably featured spring blooms, had to be planned and executed in the dead of winter. And Joe was ready with his store of sketches.

Just as Joe seldom varied his style, so he carefully followed the same methods to produce a picture throughout his entire career. On Christmas Day, 1950, just months before his death, he wrote a letter to a young man who inquired about the artist's painting procedures. Joe's description of his method is as succinct as the style the method produced.

MOUNT TOM ROAD
NEW ROCHELLE

December 25th, 50.

Mr. Ial Radom,
19 West 44th Street,
New York 18, N.Y.

Dear Mr. Radom;

   Below you will find a few hints which may prove helpful to you. This is not a formula and is not infallible as each new subject presents its own problems and difficulties.

   In doing an illustration one can often work directly from the model, whereas a cover requires more careful planning and should be designed to fill a given space on the order of a decoration. My first step is to fill a sketch pad with a number of small rough sketches about two by three inches keeping them on one sheet so you can compare them at a glance. Select the one that seems to tell the story most clearly and has an interesting design, Enlarge this by squares to the size of the magazine cover adding more detail and color as needed.

   You are now ready for the model. First make a number of pencil or charcoal studies. Select the most promising and on a sketch canvas do these in full color, oil or water with plenty of detail. Keep an open mind and be alert to capture any movement or pose that may improve your original idea.

   You may now dismiss your model, but be sure you have all the material needed with seperate studies of parts to choose from, for you are now on your own and must work entirely from your studies. This canvas will somewhat resemble a picture puzzle, and it is up to you to assemble it and fit it into your design at the same time simplify wherever possible by eliminating all unessentials, all this is done on tracing paper and retraced on the final canvas. Your finished painting may be any size to suit you, but is usually about twice the size of the reproduction.

   As a rule I start work with a round or flat sable using a thin wash with turps as a medium. Keep shadows very transparent and as the work progresses apply the paint more thickly on lighted areas adding some poppy or linseed oil if necessary, and using a larger flat bristle brush for the heavier paint, but still keeping the shadows thin and vibrant.

   When the work is dry, apply a quick drying retouching varnish either with a brush or atomizer.

   Sometimes because of prohibitive model rates or other reasons, one is forced to use photography, but try and avoid it if possible.

   With best wishes for your success.

       Sincerely

      J. C. Leyendecker

The steps are simple and hardly out of the ordinary. But Leyendecker would often work and rework or even redo a picture to achieve the best possible effect. His quest for perfection in a picture was widely known during his lifetime. A former editor for *The Saturday Evening Post* recalls that Joe always met deadlines—but just barely. A 1938 booklet celebrating the 250th anniversary of New Rochelle's founding had a cover illustration by Leyendecker of a Huguenot (page 62). Although the picture was donated to the city, and would adorn a comparatively minor, narrowly circulated booklet, Joe did eight pictures before he turned in the final painting, and admitted even then that he would have improved upon that had there been time.

Leyendecker himself once described how he left his studio on a Friday evening, having just destroyed a newly finished poster because he was not satisfied with it. He was afraid, he told a friend, that the leisurely weekend might cause him to return on Monday more tolerant of the final work than he should be.

With an annual production of dozens of magazine covers and advertisements, Joe became a wealthy man. In 1914, the brothers decided to build a home in suburban New Rochelle, then a residential mecca for many of America's foremost illustrators, and where the family had lived since 1910. They bought several acres of land on Mt. Tom Road and ordered a 14-room mansion built in the style of a French chateau. Included was a studio wing for Frank, and behind the house, a grand, formal garden, designed by Joe and planted and maintained under his supervision. (The house is now a children's day school and the grounds still show evidence of the elaborate landscaping.) The garden was Joe's passion. The time not spent pursuing his art was devoted to the garden. Included were rose and rock gardens and a Japanese garden complete with gazebo, footbridge, and waterfall. An extensive area at one end of the estate was devoted to growing fruits and vegetables, as well as raising poultry—the annual Thanksgiving *Post* cover often featured a turkey, the model for which Joe raised himself.

For several years after the completion of the mansion, Joe continued to commute to New York City. The best description of the Bryant Park studio comes from actor Neil Hamilton, a long-time friend of the artist and a model for *Post* covers (page 26) as well as Arrow Collar and other ads. In 1918, Hamilton, then unknown and seeking acting jobs, went to work as a model for Leyendecker.

The Beaux Arts Building across from Bryant Park, Sixth Avenue at 40th Street in New York City, as it looked when Leyendecker occupied an eighth-floor studio from 1907 to 1920.

"I was making the rounds of the many film studios in Fort Lee, New Jersey, when a fellow actor pointed out Charles Beach to me on the lot and identified the dapper gentleman as the real Arrow Collar Man." Since the competition for film parts was great even in that day, Hamilton was prompted to offer himself as an artist's model. Learning that Leyendecker had a studio at Bryant Park, the actor presented himself there one afternoon. "My knock on the door was answered by a butler in full uniform who asked me to come in and sit in the foyer. In a few minutes I was ushered into the studio which looked somewhat like a small Grand Central Station. Leyendecker was a fairly small person, but intensely attractive. He seemed to listen intently to every word I said. I told him I never worked as a model but was willing to learn. He asked me to stand up, put one foot on the chair and hold my left hand over my eye as though seeing a ship land." The short audition was acceptable, and Hamilton was employed at $6 per day, plus lunch.

Almost twenty years later, two 11-year-old boys recorded their experiences as Leyendecker models for the July Fourth *Post* cover of 1937 (page 26). Howard Davenport, Jr. (the boy on top) posed first: "Where the sign was supposed to be we had a high chair. The lamppost was really a studio lamp. I got tired of holding my arm up as if I were waving, so Mr. Leyendecker gave me a studio lamp to hang on to. The sweater, red in the picture, was really brown, and he changed my shoes in the picture too." Earl Williams, who also appeared in a previous Thanksgiving cover, recalled Leyendecker's only instructions were "to look down as if I was scared, and to grab hold of the lamp and sit on the high chair." The boys posed for several sessions of sketches as well as for production of the final picture.

World War I produced the last great body of posters in America. In 1917 Leyendecker joined such outstanding illustrators as Charles Dana Gibson, Howard Chandler Christie, Maxfield Parrish, James Montgomery Flagg, and N.C. Wyeth in working for the Division of Pictorial Publicity of the U.S. Navy, the first U.S. government department to commission and issue posters during the war. Working under Lt. Commander Henry Reuterdahl, Leyendecker created posters for naval recruitment and for the U.S. Fuel Administration, depicting such warnings as "Order Coal Now" (page 76). Gibson was the chairman of the local New York illustrators group, and he distributed assignments at regular luncheon meetings convened at a 36th Street restaurant.

Following the war, Leyendecker gave up his New York City studio to work out of the New Rochelle mansion. He ordered an extra wing built on the side of the house opposite from the studio in which Frank worked.

In the early twenties, tensions at the mansion began to mount and relationships deteriorate. Details of the circumstances and the bad feelings that resulted are not known. But in 1923 Frank and Augusta, who sided with him during the family crisis, left the Mt. Tom Road mansion.

Whatever problems existed for Frank at the Leyendecker home were compounded by his increasing dissatisfaction with his work. He found it difficult to complete assignments, and because of this, it became more difficult to get new ones. Once he even admitted to a model that he purposely painted out-of-proportion figures for one company because he was not given the freedom to work as he wished. He was consistently behind in his portion of the mortgage payments on the estate and with his share of the upkeep. Beach paid Frank's share on a number of occasions.

After the rift, Frank took a one-room garage apartment-studio in New Rochelle not far from the mansion. He painted only sporadically and was noticeably depressed at the treatment he received from his brother. In *My Adventures as an Illustrator*, Rockwell reports that Frank took drugs during this period. If this is so, it may have been the drugs, coupled with acute depression, that caused his death at age 47 on Good Friday, 1924.

Joe was profoundly disturbed at his brother's death only a month after his fiftieth birthday. Those who knew him could see how deeply the loss troubled him. He became remote—but not a hermit. He still went out on frequent driving junkets, attended artists' group meetings, and taught at Pickett. In 1927 when the artist Coles Phillips died, he invited Phillips' widow and family to the mansion, where they stayed for several months. He enjoyed regular visits to Grand Isle Casino—his bedroom overlooked the famous Casino and the bright lights and music drew him there many summer evenings.

The twenties were professionally a good period for Leyendecker. He was doing more clothing ads than ever and a record number of *Post* covers. *The Post* began to use four-color printing in 1926, and this added dimension stimulated Joe to create pictures with even more verve than that shown in his previous work printed

Frank Leyendecker in his new studio at the Mt. Tom Road mansion, New Rochelle, New York, 1915. Courtesy Mrs. James F. Parr.

Works of Frank X. Leyendecker: (left) "An End Run," illustration for The Century Illustrated Monthly Magazine, November 1909; (right) watercolor of a chateau near Paris, 1897; Navy recruitment poster, 1918. Courtesy Metropolitan Museum of Art. Photo Stephen Klain.

The rose garden.

Back entrance.

Studio wing, added in 1920.

Front entrance.

The Leyendecker mansion on Mt. Tom Road, New Rochelle, as it looked in the 1930s. Courtesy Mrs. James F. Parr.

in black, white, and red. (He often painted his early *Post* covers in full color anyway, even though they would never be seen like that.) The pert, flip attitudes of the decade called for at least a partial break with the human interest pictures so popular in preceding years. It was no longer enough to serve up a boy with a puppy or a woman radiant in a new Easter bonnet to entice readers. The times demanded more sophisticated pictures, and Leyendecker supplied them. *The Post* continued, of course, to favor such themes as strong patriotism, traditional celebration of holidays, and the promise of a brighter future.

Although Leyendecker's pictures had made him one of the country's most popular illustrators, America during the years between the Armistice and the Wall Street Crash was even more receptive to the people the artist portrayed. The Leyendecker men and women were certainly not a part of what is now called "Flaming Youth." While John Held, Jr. delighted the era with his caricatures of flappers and sheiks, Leyendecker subjects were of another world—but one still widely understood and admired. The characters of F. Scott Fitzgerald's *The Great Gatsby* come to mind in many Leyendecker pictures of the twenties: well-to-do, civilized people with self-confidence reinforced by breeding, education, position, and taste. They were sophisticated but not above gaiety, tolerant but aloof, and quietly scornful of many. These are the same beautiful people who caught imaginations in previous decades, but in the twenties the public was extraordinarily receptive to them.

Perhaps a Leyendecker contemporary like F. Scott Fitzgerald—although much more identified with a specific era than Leyendecker is—can best express the essence of Leyendecker's work. Fitzgerald's description of Beatrice in his 1920 novel *This Side of Paradise* puts into words the same sensibilities Leyendecker portrayed in many of his most admired pictures:

"All in all Beatrice O'Hara absorbed the sort of education that will be quite impossible ever again; a tutelage measured by the number of things and people one could be contemptuous of and charming about; a culture rich in all arts and traditions, barren of all ideas, in the last of those days when the great gardener clipped the inferior roses to produce one perfect bud."

The Depression did not affect Joe severely. He had never saved enough money to invest. But in that bleak period, he lost many of his major clients: the Arrow Man

Leyendecker in his rock garden at the New Rochelle mansion, ca. 1940. Courtesy Mrs. James F. Parr.

was gone, as were the ads for Kuppenheimer and other clothiers. *The Saturday Evening Post* covers reflected the hopes of Americans, many of whom had reached their lowest point. Elaborately decorated pictures of fantasy and escapism predominated, and in the mid-1930s Joe could still earn $50,000 in a good year.

However, by the end of the decade, Leyendecker was called upon less often to do *Post* covers. When Ben Hibbs took over as editor of *The Post* in 1941, he decided to make over the magazine; he changed the logo and terminated many of the authors and illustrators whom *The Post* had used for years. Leyendecker's work had not declined in quality, but he was, the editor said, too strongly associated with *The Post* that was. If the magazine were to remain a viable publication, a new image was needed.

Leyendecker found himself in difficult financial circumstances from the years during World War II until his death in 1951. His theory that an artist should spend to keep himself producing had backfired. Approaching the age of 70, Leyendecker had earned and spent a fortune. Now he was faced with diminished income and upkeep on a huge estate as well as support of his sister Augusta. Leyendecker was forced to dismiss the large house and garden staff. It became necessary for him to actively seek work for the first time in decades to keep the mansion and gardens, now maintained solely by Beach and himself.

Although circumstances were tough, they were hardly desperate, and Leyendecker held onto the estate. He painted war bond posters of outstanding American military leaders for The Timken Company during the war (pages 79–80); he secured a few calendar illustration jobs; and he was hired to do covers for *The American Weekly,* the Hearst Sunday supplement magazine (page 202). He appeared regularly in *The American Weekly,* and there continued his famous New Year babies.

But Joe was tired by this time, too much so to be very imaginative. He repeated many of the themes done for *Post* covers, often changing just enough detail to avoid blatant repetition. The pictures were poorly reproduced by the publication, and in many instances the quality is sadly below the usual high standards Joe demanded in better days.

Leyendecker had been working on the 1952 *American Weekly* New Year's cover, and was sitting with Beach on the back terrace overlooking his gardens when he had a heart attack and died on July 25, 1951, at 77 years of age. The estate, consisting of the house, land, and hundreds of pictures, but only valued at $60,000, was willed to Augusta and Beach, to be divided equally. The real estate was sold. Because Joe kept a clause in his contracts, when possible, that paintings were to be returned to him after their use, the collection of pictures represented a lifetime of work. Most of them were sold by Beach at an outdoor auction on the grounds of the estate. The hundreds of magazine covers were priced at a mere $75. The sketch canvases, which Joe had wanted destroyed at his death, were sold for $25 each, or cut into pieces by Beach and sold for $2 to $5 each. Artists and Leyendecker-admirers from all over the East rummaged through the tables of pictures, and the lot was disposed of quickly.

Beach, an old man himself by this time—and deeply affected by the loss of Joe—moved to a rooming house in New Rochelle. He was known in his later years as a heavy drinker, and within a short time he too died, having spent most of his money on nightly drinking bouts.

Augusta, the last of the Leyendecker family, died at a residential hotel in New York City in 1957, surrounded by the few pictures painted by her brothers that she had not had to sell.

CHRONOLOGY

J.C. Leyendecker, 1874–1951

March 23, 1874. Born at Montabour, Germany. Named Joseph Christian Leyendecker. Son of Peter and Elizabeth Ortseifen Leyendecker.

1877. Brother Frank Xavier Leyendecker born at Montabour.

1882. Leyendecker family emigrated to Chicago.

1889. Apprenticed to J. Manz & Company, an engraving house, Monroe Street, Chicago.

September 1889. Began study at Chicago Art Institute; instructed by John H. Vanderpoel. Continued studies through 1894.

1894. Completed 60 illustrations for an edition of *The Bible* printed by Manz.

1895. Created cover and illustrations for two novels: *Dolly Dialogues* by Anthony Hope Hawkins and *One Fair Daughter* by Frank F. Moore.

August 1896. Won first prize in *The Century* magazine's Midsummer Holiday Number Contest; painting used by *The Century* as the cover.

September 1896. Left Chicago for Paris with brother Frank to begin two years of art study at the Académie Julian and Colarossi.

January–December 1897. Created the twelve pictures used on the covers of the monthly *Inland Printer,* published in Chicago.

April. One-man exhibition at Salon Champs du Mars in Paris.

August. Returned from Paris to Chicago.

September. Opened first studio with brother Frank in Chicago's Stock Exchange Building.

November 1898. First cover for *Collier's* magazine, Thanksgiving Issue. First of 48 *Collier's* covers, 1898–1918.

May 1899. First cover illustration for *The Saturday Evening Post.* First of 322 *Post* covers, 1899–1943.

1900. Closed Chicago studio. Leyendecker brothers moved to New York City and opened a studio at 7 East 32nd Street.

1901. Illustrated "The Rubaiyat of Omar Khayyam" for *Delineator Magazine.* First met Charles Beach with whom he lived for 50 years.

1905. Commissioned by Cluett, Peabody & Co., Inc., manufacturer of Arrow Collars, to do first Arrow Collar Man advertisement. Created Arrow Collar Man image, 1905–1930.

December 1905. Illustrated "A Song of Faith" (Twenty-Third Psalm) for *Delineator Magazine*.

1906. Illustrated Egerton R. Williams' novel *Ridolfo, the Coming of the Dawn*.

December 1906. Created first New Year's cherub for *The Saturday Evening Post*.

1907. Moved to house near Washington Square in Greenwich Village and opened studio in Beaux Arts Building, Sixth Avenue at 40th Street.

1908. Began work for B. Kuppenheimer & Company and Interwoven Socks.

1910. Moved from New York City to New Rochelle, New York. Maintained New York City studio at 40th Street.

1912. First of a series of advertisements for Kellogg's Corn Flakes.

1914. Built the mansion on Mt. Tom Road, New Rochelle.

1917–1919. Contributed war posters for Division of Pictorial Publicity of the U.S. Navy and U.S. Fuel Administration.

1920. Gave up the 40th Street studio to work in a newly built studio at his New Rochelle home.

April 1924. Death of brother Frank X. Leyendecker.

April 1926. First four-color cover for *The Saturday Evening Post*.

January 1943. Last cover for *The Saturday Evening Post*.

1944. Series of war bond posters depicting American military leaders, commissioned by The Timken Company.

December 1945. First cover for *The American Weekly* magazine.

July 25, 1951. Died at New Rochelle, New York. Age 77.

ILLUSTRATIONS

Although J.C. Leyendecker was one of the country's leading illustrators in America's "Golden Age of Illustration," the pictures he drew to illuminate textual material are a minor aspect of his early work. He illustrated a few books and a handful of magazine stories and poems—well represented on the following pages—during the first sixteen years (1894–1910) of his long career and even then just sporadically. As his fame and the demand for his work grew, Leyendecker preferred doing advertising art and magazine covers that received wider exposure. Although Leyendecker's early *Saturday Evening Post* covers commissioned by editor George Horace Lorimer illustrated stories inside the issue, the vast number of Leyendecker's 322 *Post* covers had more general themes and were illustrations only in the sense that he conceptualized themes such as "Spring," "Christmas," and "New Year's." After 1910 Leyendecker only created art for special magazine stories—for example, a *Saturday Evening Post* article by President Herbert Hoover and a *Post* cover story on Will Rogers (page 201).

David and Goliath.

Saul's Suicide.

The Fugitive King.

David's Charge to Solomon.

Illustrations for The Bible, *Powers Brothers Company, Chicago, 1894.*

Title page.

Sigmund's Love Song.

Siegfried's Song.

Recitative and Song to the Evening Star.

Illustrations for "Love Songs from the Wagner Operas," *The Century* magazine, 1902(?).

The Duet of Brynhilda and Siegfried.

Brynhilda's Immolation.

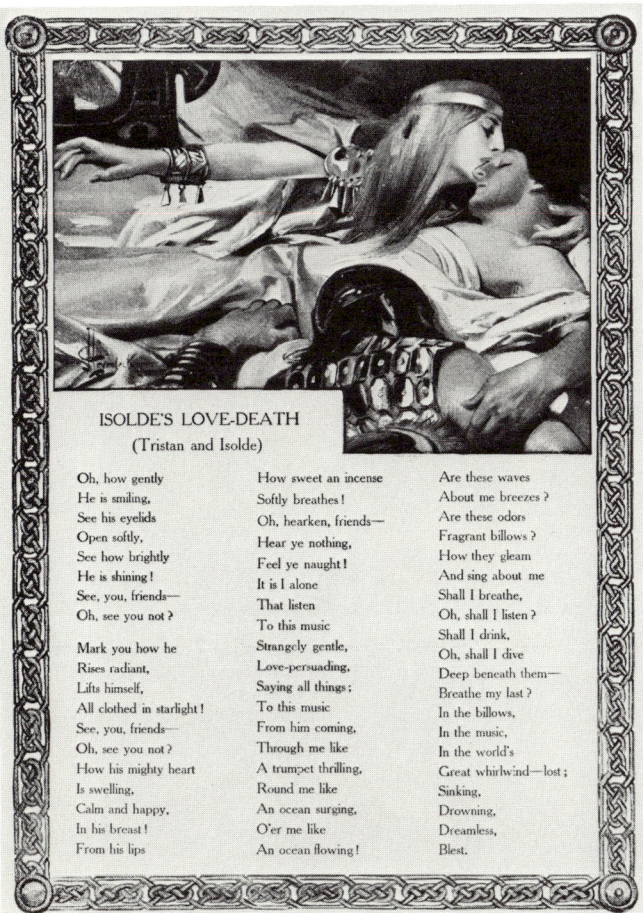

Isolde's Love-Death.

Series courtesy Stephen R. Sanderson collection.

Back piece.

Illustration for R.D. Paine's "A Victory Unforeseen," Scribner's *magazine, Harvard-Yale Boat Race Issue, July 1905.*

Illustrations for Alfred Domett's "The Great Guest Comes" (or "A Christmas Hymn"), <u>The Century</u> magazine, Christmas Number, December 1905. Series courtesy Stephen R. Sanderson collection.

Illustration for Egerton R. Williams, Jr.'s novel Ridolfo, the Coming of the Dawn, *1906. Courtesy Stephen R. Sanderson collection.*

Illustration for Charles B. Hudson's novel The Crimson Conquest, *1907.*

Frontispiece.

Illustration 1.

Illustration 2.

Illustration 3.

Illustrations for "A Song of Faith" (The Twenty-Third Psalm), <u>Delineator Magazine</u>, December 1905.

Illustration 4.

Illustration 5.

Illustration 6.

Back piece.

"Queen Meave," from Theodore Roosevelt's "The Ancient Irish Sagas," <u>The Century</u> magazine, January 1907. Courtesy Stephen R. Sanderson collection.

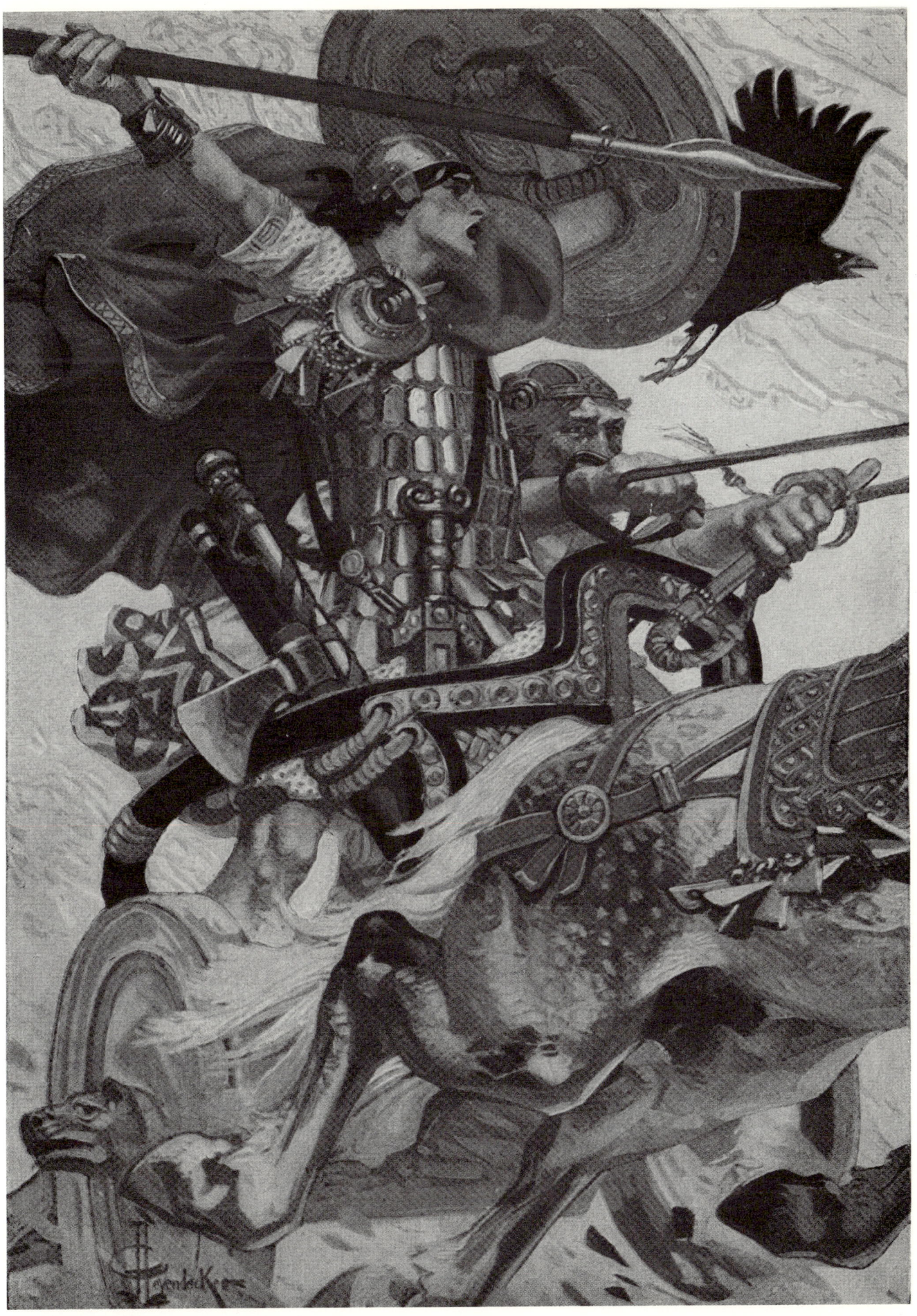
"Cuchulain in Battle," from Theodore Roosevelt's "The Ancient Irish Sagas," The Century magazine, January 1907. Courtesy Stephen R. Sanderson collection.

"The Huguenot," frontispiece, 250th Anniversary Commemorative Booklet, New Rochelle, New York, 1938.

POSTERS

That portion of Leyendecker's career devoted to creating posters was relatively short, and except for special designs commissioned during World Wars I and II, it was limited—like his illustration work—to his earliest years. The small number of posters in Leyendecker's art is partly explained by the fact that posters were far less popular in America than in Europe; a major career could not be built on poster work. However, there is a fine line between the poster as an advertising medium and the art for magazine ads. Leyendecker's success for more than half a century came with his magazine ad art, a more practical and far-reaching form of advertising than posters.

Poster for Frank F. Moore's novel One Fair Daughter, May 1895. (Artist's name incorrectly spelled.) Courtesy Columbia University Library. Photo Geoffrey Clements.

The Century magazine's poster for the Midsummer Holiday Number, August 1896. Courtesy Columbia University Library. Photo Geoffrey Clements.

The Inland Printer magazine poster, October 1897. Courtesy Columbia University Library. Photo Geoffrey Clements.

The Chap-Book magazine poster, 1899. Courtesy Columbia University Library. Photo Geoffrey Clements.

Up To Date magazine poster, 1899. Courtesy Columbia University Library. Photo Geoffrey Clements.

Up To Date magazine poster, 1899. Courtesy Columbia University Library. Photo Geoffrey Clements.

Up To Date magazine poster, 1899. Courtesy Columbia University Library. Photo Geoffrey Clements.

Success magazine poster for the Christmas Number, 1900. Courtesy Columbia University Library. Photo Geoffrey Clements.

"Rowing," <u>Scribner's</u> magazine poster, 1906. Courtesy Columbia University Library. Photo Geoffrey Clements.

Poster for University of Pennsylvania, 1906. Courtesy Columbia University Library. Photo Geoffrey Clements.

"Weapons for Liberty," war bonds poster, 1917.

"Order Coal Now," poster for U.S. Fuel Administration, 1917.

U.S. Navy recruitment poster, 1918.

"Enlist Today, U.S. Marines," 1918. Courtesy Columbia University Library. Photo Geoffrey Clements.

"General MacArthur," war bonds poster, 1944. Courtesy The Timken Company.

"General Eisenhower," war bonds poster, 1944. Courtesy The Timken Company.

ADVERTISEMENTS

Leyendecker's reputation as an illustrator was based largely on the images he created for product advertisement, and it was as an ad artist that Leyendecker was most prolific. During the first three decades of this century he produced designs for as varied a list of products as soap, breakfast cereal, and automobiles. But his most famous, and by far most popular, pictures were those created for menswear advertisements, particularly Arrow Collar, B. Kuppenheimer, and Hart Schaffner & Marx. The enormous impact on the American public caused by these illustrations of handsome, stylishly dressed men may be difficult to understand today: the "Arrow Collar Man" became the standard against which all American males were measured. The esteem in which these Leyendecker creations were held during the first three decades of this century is reflected in F. Scott Fitzgerald's 1929 story "The Last of the Belles," in which Ailie Calhoun's brother is her ideal: "She showed me his picture—it was a handsome, earnest face with a Leyendecker forelock —and told me that when she met someone who measured up to him she'd marry."

McAvoy Malt-Marrow advertisement, 1899. Courtesy Chicago Historical Society.

Pierce Arrow advertisement, 1909. Courtesy Pierce Rice collection.

Arrow Collars and Shirts advertisement. Courtesy Cluett, Peabody & Co., Inc.

The House of Kuppenheimer advertisement, 1918. Courtesy Alex Chasky collection.

Cover design for The House of Kuppenheimer 1918 Style Book.

Pictures for The House of Kuppenheimer 1918 Style Book.

The House of Kuppenheimer advertisements.

Arrow Collars and Shirts advertisement, 1912. Courtesy Pierce Rice collection.

Arrow Collar advertisement, 1912.

Arrow Collars and Shirts advertisement, 1913. Courtesy Pierce Rice collection.

Arrow Collars and Shirts advertisement, 1913.

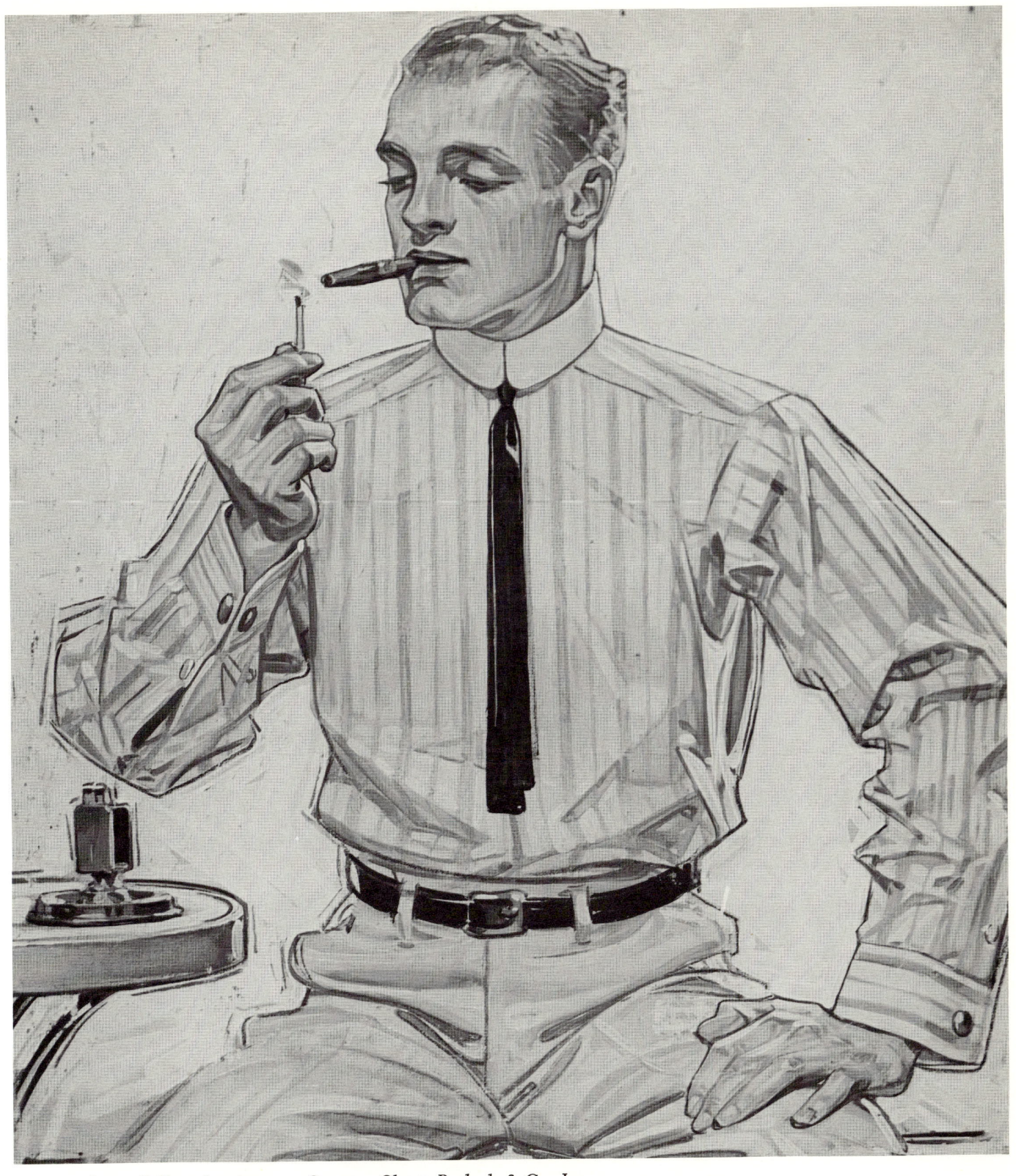
Arrow Collar advertisement. Courtesy Cluett, Peabody & Co., Inc.

Arrow Collars and Shirts advertisement, 1913.

Overland Automobile advertisement, 1914.

grasp what 50,000 cars a year means. They can-
numerous and various manufacturing economies,
normous production effects.
ill but compare the $950 Overland with most any
$1400 cars they will be unable to find much

er 3000 Overland dealers. Look up the one in
mine this car carefully.
14 catalogue and name of nearest dealer on request.
Please address Dept. 26.

$950

COMPLETELY EQUIPPED
With Electric Starter and Generator, $1075, F. O. B. Toledo.
Canadian Prices: F. O. B. Toledo, $1250 Completely
Equipped. Duty paid. $1425 with electric starter and generator. Duty paid.

The House of Kuppenheimer advertisement, 1917. Courtesy Alex Chasky collection.

"Over the Top," The House of Kuppenheimer advertisement. Courtesy Alex Chasky collection.

Ivory Soap advertisement, 1900. Courtesy Procter & Gamble Company.

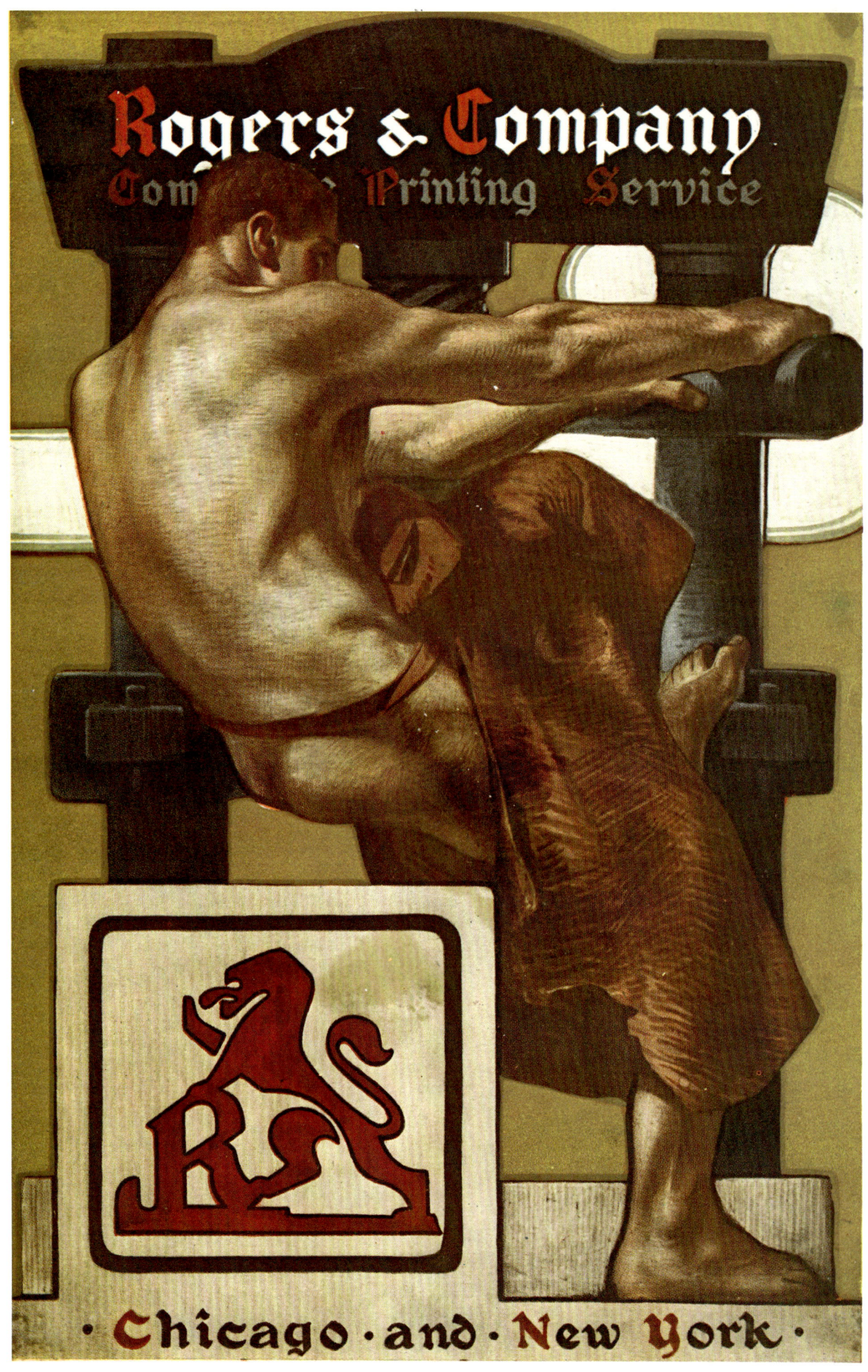

Rogers & Company Printers advertisement, 1900. Courtesy Stephen R. Sanderson collection.

Kellogg's Corn Flakes advertisement, 1917. Courtesy The Kellogg Company.

Arrow Collar advertisement, 1910. Courtesy Cluett, Peabody & Co., Inc.

Arrow Collar advertisement, ca. 1913. Courtesy Cluett, Peabody & Co., Inc.

Arrow Collar advertisement. Courtesy Cluett, Peabody & Co., Inc.

Arrow Collar advertisement. Courtesy Cluett, Peabody & Co., Inc.

Arrow Collar advertisement, ca. 1922. Courtesy Cluett, Peabody & Co., Inc.

B. Kuppenheimer & Company advertisement. Courtesy Stephen R. Sanderson collection.

Arrow Collar advertisement, 1912. Courtesy Cluett, Peabody & Co., Inc.

Arrow Collar advertisements. Courtesy Cluett, Peabody & Co., Inc.

Arrow Collar advertisement, 1929. Courtesy Cluett, Peabody & Co., Inc.

B. *Kuppenheimer & Company advertisement.*

The House of Kuppenheimer advertisement, 1918. Courtesy Alex Chasky collection.

The House of Kuppenheimer advertisement. Courtesy Alex Chasky collection.

The House of Kuppenheimer advertisement, 1918. The picture-within-the-picture is an 1899 advertisement that Leyendecker d for A.B. Kirschbaum, a Chicago clothier. Courtesy Alex Chasky collection.

The House of Kuppenheimer advertisement, 1921. Courtesy Pierce Rice collection.

The House of Kuppenheimer advertisement, 1921. Courtesy Pierce Rice collection.

Interwoven Socks advertisement, 1927. Courtesy The Interwoven Company.

Interwoven Socks advertisement, 1924. Courtesy The Interwoven Company.

Interwoven Socks advertisement, 1924. Courtesy The Interwoven Company.

The House of Kuppenheimer advertisement, 1922. Courtesy Pierce Rice collection.

Chesterfield Cigarettes advertisements, 1918. Courtesy Liggett & Myers, Inc., and the Metropolitan Museum of Art. Photos Stephen Klain.

Arrow Collar advertisement. Courtesy Cluett, Peabody & Co., Inc.

The House of Kuppenheimer advertisement, 1930. Courtesy Stephen R. Sanderson collection.

Arrow Collars and Shirts advertisement, 1930. Courtesy Stephen R. Sanderson collection.

MAGAZINE COVERS

In a career that spanned more than fifty years, Leyendecker created over 500 paintings for magazine covers. The artist's first cover for a national magazine was in 1896, designed originally as a poster for *The Century* magazine poster contest (page 66). In 1897, Leyendecker drew a series of twelve covers that appeared on *The Inland Printer* that year (pages 129, 161). The next year he sold his first cover to *Collier's,* and in the twenty years that followed, Leyendecker produced 48 *Collier's* covers. Leyendecker painted his first *Saturday Evening Post* cover in 1899 (page 26), and he continued to work for the magazine until 1943. He created 322 covers for *The Post,* and in some years as many as a dozen designs by the artist were featured by *The Post*. The reason for Leyendecker's success was that his pictures spoke to and for millions of Americans. The reputation gained as a result of his magazine covers established Leyendecker as one of America's most popular illustrators.

The Inland Printer cover, December 1897. Courtesy Columbia University Library. Photo Geoffrey Clements.

Success magazine cover, April 1903.

Success magazine cover, June 1904.

Success magazine cover, December 1905.

"When Shall We Fly?" Collier's *cover, February 23, 1907.*

"Westward Ho!" Collier's cover, December 7, 1907.

Success Magazine cover, February 1908.

The Popular Magazine cover, March 1909.

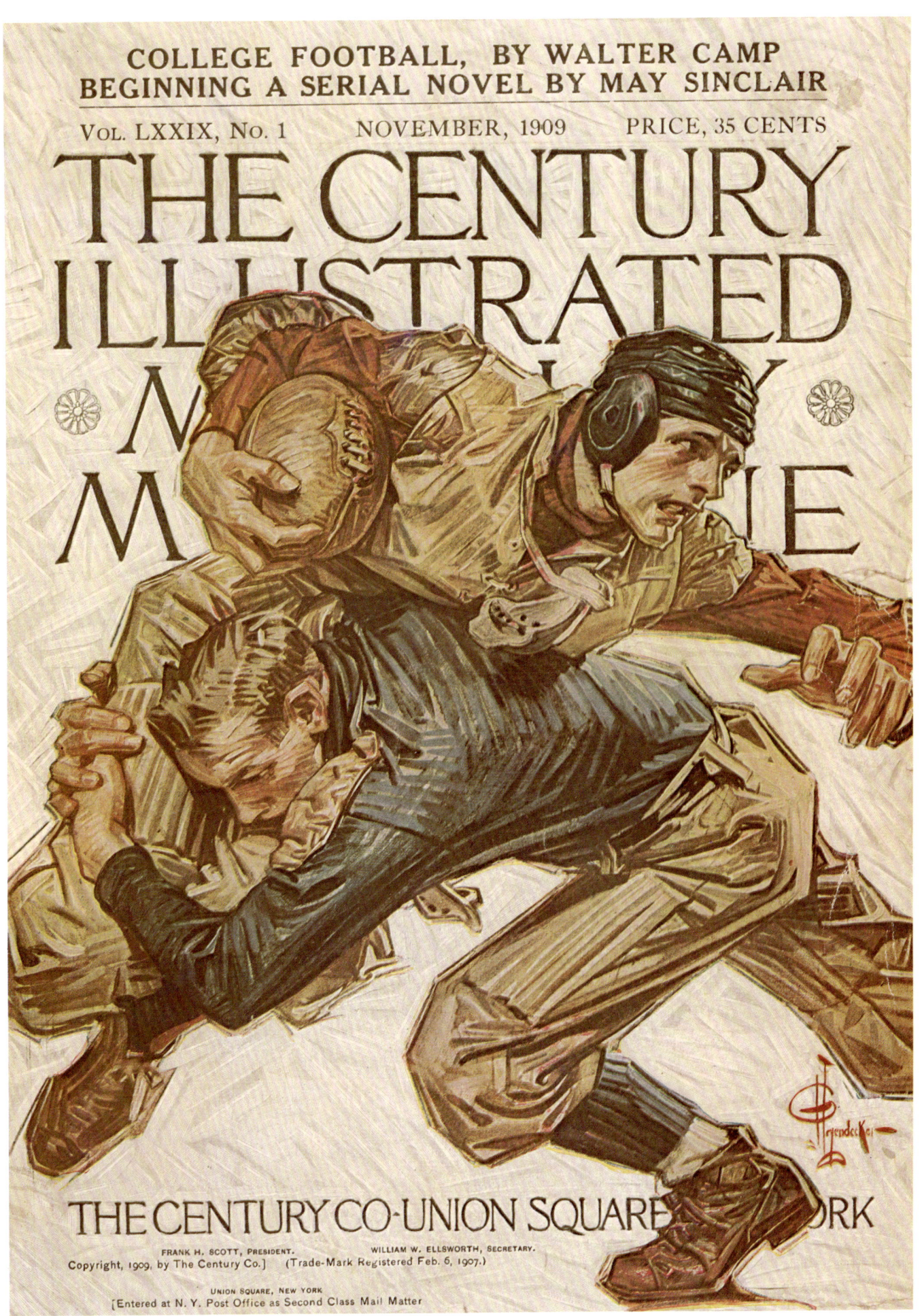

"College Football," The Century Illustrated Monthly Magazine cover, November 1909.

The Saturday Evening Post cover, April 3, 1926. First four-color cover by Leyendecker for The Post. Courtesy Curtis Publishing Company.

The Saturday Evening Post cover, November 26, 1927. Courtesy Curtis Publishing Company.

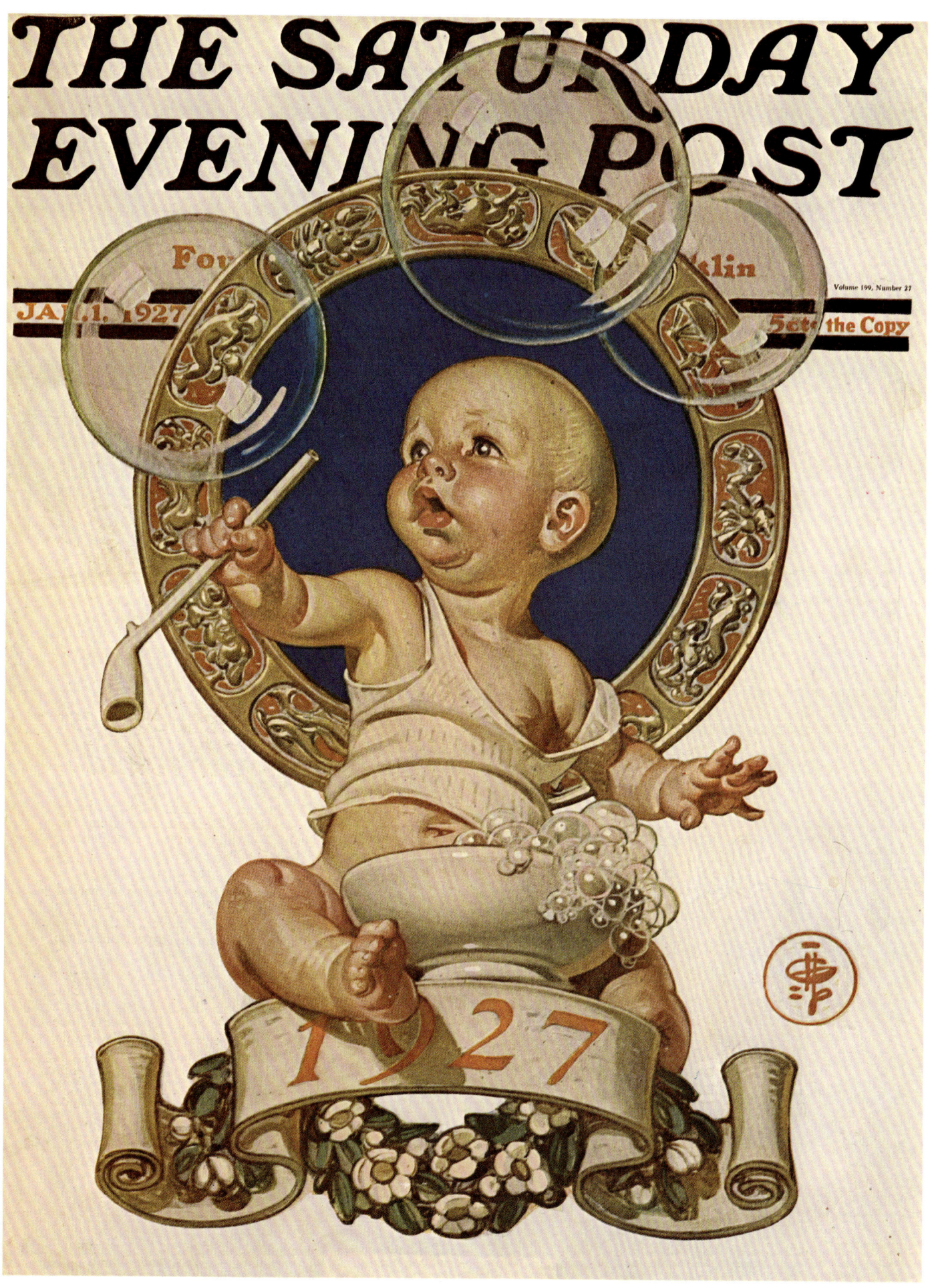

The Saturday Evening Post cover, January 1, 1927. Courtesy Curtis Publishing Company.

The Saturday Evening Post cover, June 2, 1928. Courtesy Curtis Publishing Company.

The Saturday Evening Post cover, November 24, 1928. Courtesy Curtis Publishing Company.

The Saturday Evening Post cover, June 29, 1929. Courtesy Curtis Publishing Company.

The Saturday Evening Post cover, June 8, 1929. Courtesy Curtis Publishing Company.

The Saturday Evening Post cover, July 4, 1931. Courtesy Curtis Publishing Company.

The Saturday Evening Post cover, June 4, 1932. Courtesy Curtis Publishing Company.

The Saturday Evening Post cover, August 6, 1932. Courtesy Curtis Publishing Company.

The Saturday Evening Post cover, December 31, 1932. Courtesy Curtis Publishing Company.

The Saturday Evening Post cover, December 23, 1933. Courtesy Curtis Publishing Company.

The Saturday Evening Post cover, March 31, 1934. Courtesy Curtis Publishing Company.

The Saturday Evening Post cover, July 7, 1934. Courtesy Curtis Publishing Company.

The Saturday Evening Post cover, September 15, 1934. Courtesy Curtis Publishing Company.

The Saturday Evening Post cover, December 29, 1934. Courtesy Curtis Publishing Company.

The Saturday Evening Post cover, February 23, 1935. Courtesy Curtis Publishing Company.

The Saturday Evening Post cover, October 19, 1935. Courtesy Curtis Publishing Company.

The Saturday Evening Post cover, February 15, 1936. Courtesy Curtis Publishing Company.

The Saturday Evening Post cover, April 11, 1936. Courtesy Curtis Publishing Company.

The Saturday Evening Post cover, March 27, 1937. Courtesy Curtis Publishing Company.

The Saturday Evening Post cover, January 20, 1940. Courtesy Curtis Publishing Company.

Painting for The American Weekly magazine cover, November 24, 1946.

The Inland Printer covers, 1897. Courtesy Columbia University Library. Photo Geoffrey Clements.

Chicago Evening Post cover, Book Number, 1898. Courtesy Columbia University Library. Photo Geoffrey Clements.

The Inland Printer cover, Easter Number, March 1899.

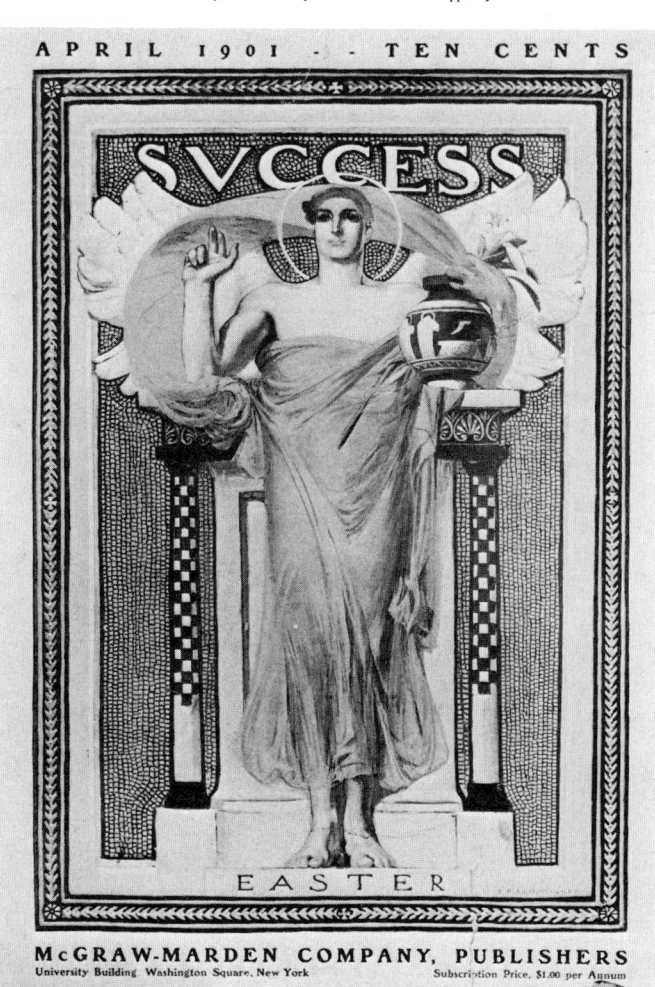

Success magazine cover, Easter Number, April 1901. Courtesy Chicago Historical Society.

Success magazine cover, Thanksgiving Number, November 1901.

Success magazine cover, August 1902. Courtesy Chicago His

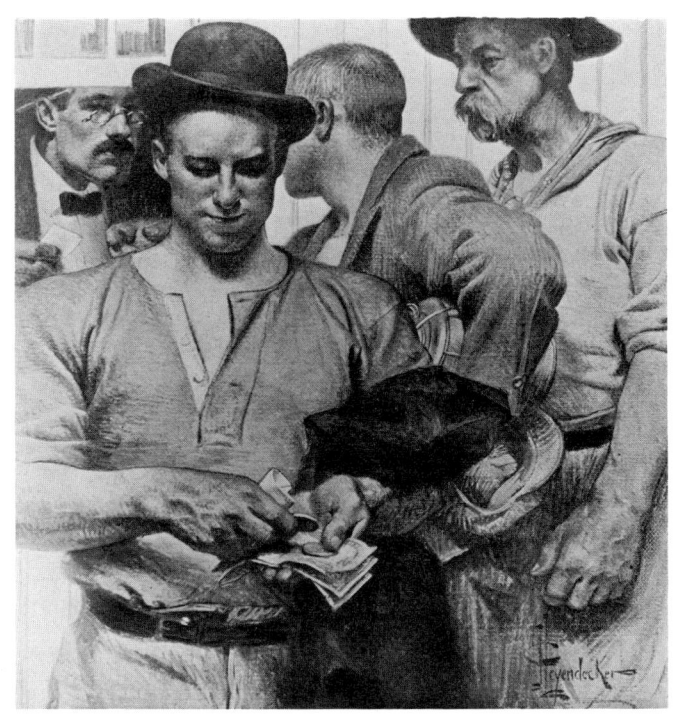

Collier's covers, 1904–1907.

Painting for Collier's cover, August 28, 1909.

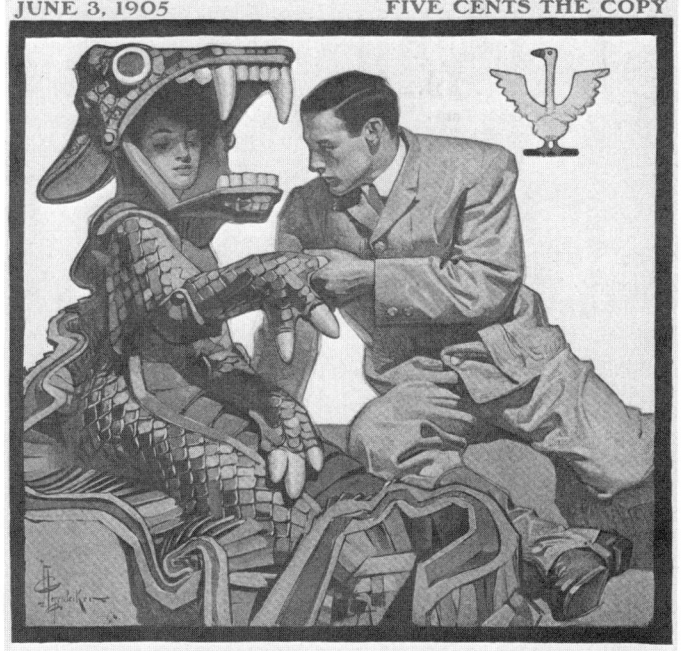

The Saturday Evening Post covers, 1903–1905. Courtesy Curtis Publishing Company.

The Saturday Evening Post covers, 1906–1907. Courtesy Curtis Publishing Company.

The Saturday Evening Post cover, July 20, 1907. Courtesy Curtis Publishing Company.

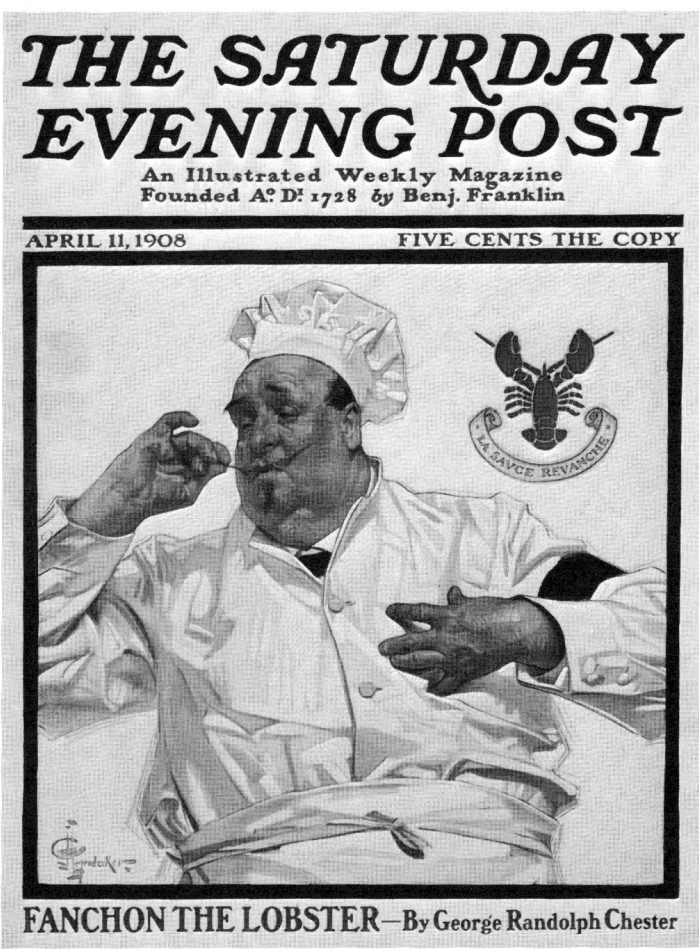
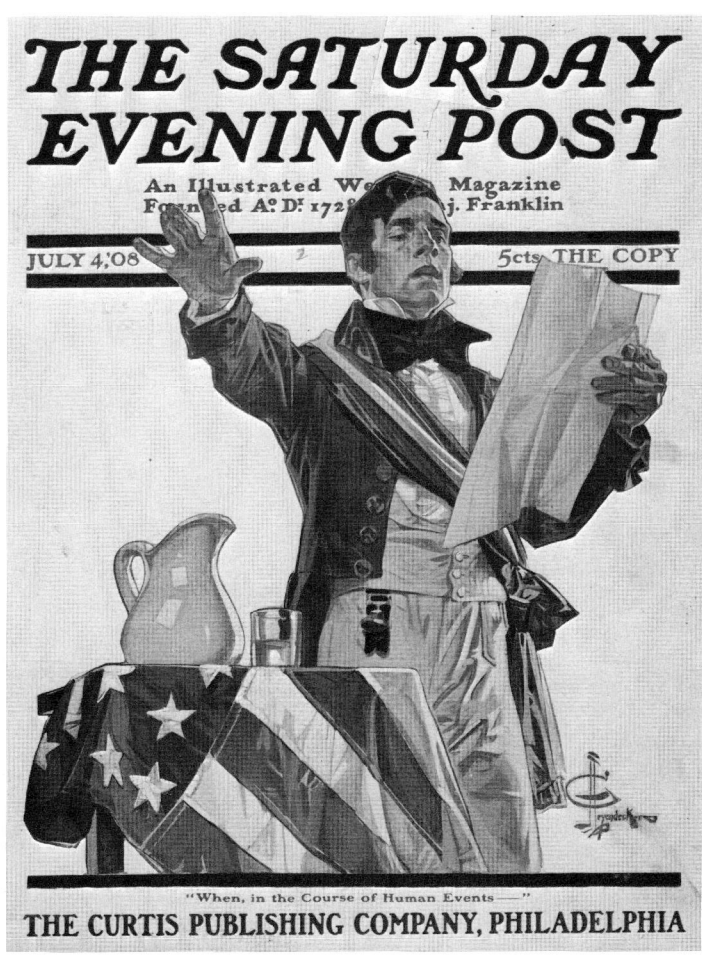

The Saturday Evening Post covers, 1907–1908. Courtesy Curtis Publishing Company.

Collier's cover, August 17, 1907.

The Saturday Evening Post covers, 1908–1909. Courtesy Curtis Publishing Company.

The Saturday Evening Post covers, 1909–1910. Courtesy Curtis Publishing Company.

The Saturday Evening Post cover, December 31, 1910. Courtesy Curtis Publishing Company.

The Popular Magazine covers, 1909–1910.

The Pittsburgh Dispatch Monthly Magazine cover, June 12, 1910.

Judge magazine cover, January 28, 1911.

The Saturday Evening Post cover, February 25, 1911. Courtesy Curtis Publishing Company.

The Saturday Evening Post covers, 1911–1912. Courtesy Curtis Publishing Company.

The Saturday Evening Post cover, March 22, 1913. Courtesy Curtis Publishing Company.

The Saturday Evening Post covers, 1913. Courtesy Curtis Publishing Company.

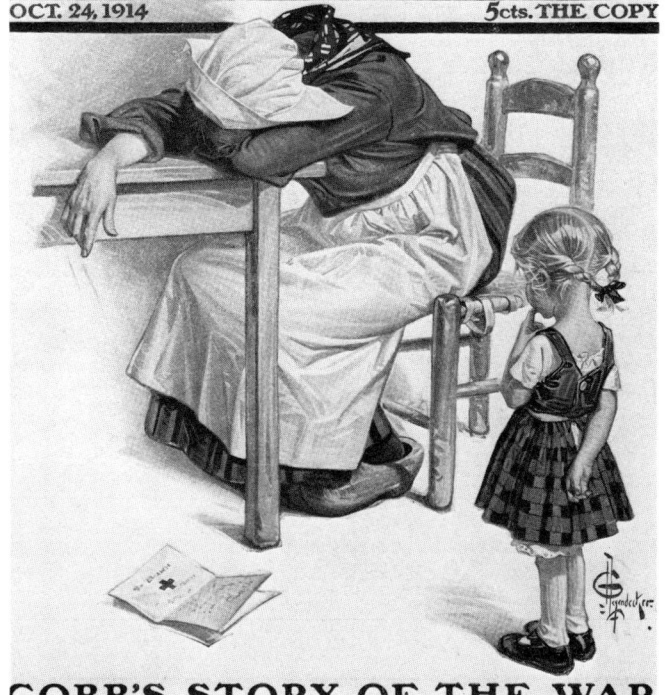

The Saturday Evening Post covers, 1914. Courtesy Curtis Publishing Company.

Collier's covers, 1914.

The Saturday Evening Post covers, 1915. Courtesy Curtis Publishing Company.

The Saturday Evening Post cover, November 20, 1915. Courtesy Curtis Publishing Company.

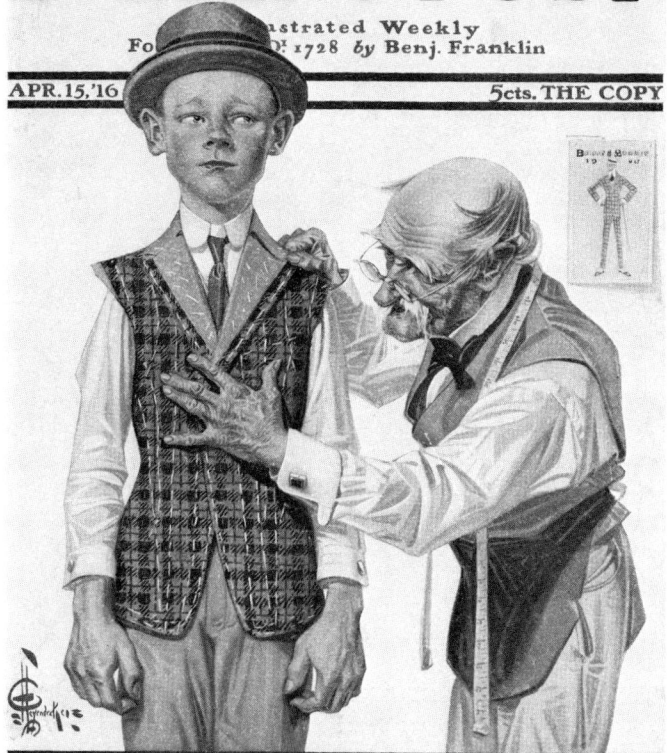

The Saturday Evening Post covers, 1916–1917. Courtesy Curtis Publishing Company.

The Saturday Evening Post covers, 1917–1918. Courtesy Curtis Publishing Company.

The Saturday Evening Post cover, April 5, 1919. Courtesy Curtis Publishing Company.

The Saturday Evening Post covers, 1919. Courtesy Curtis Publishing Company.

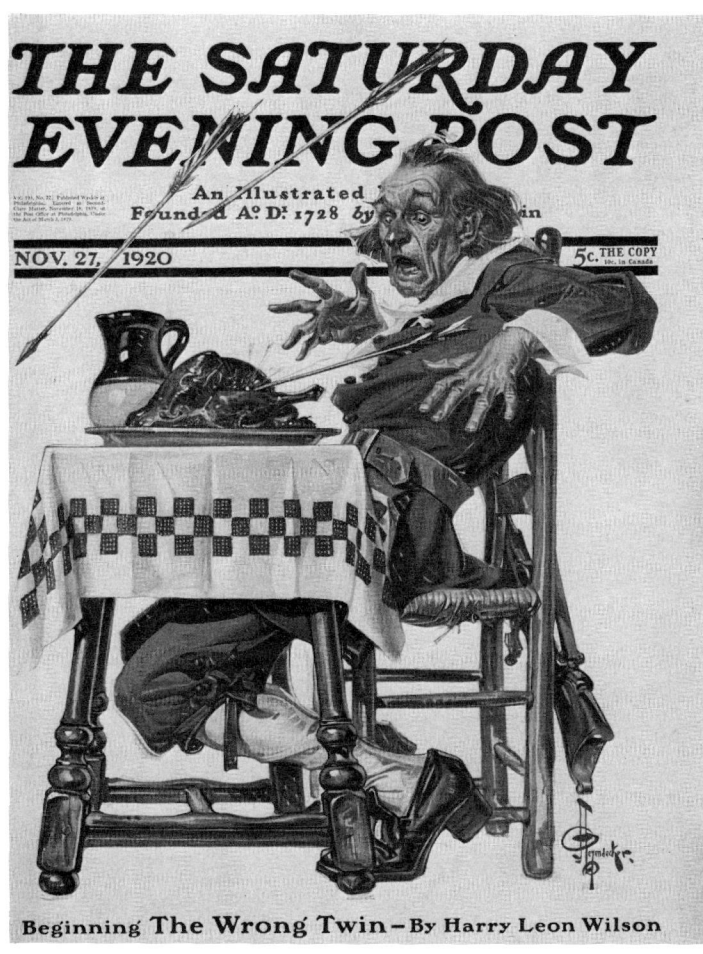

The Saturday Evening Post covers, 1920–1921. Courtesy Curtis Publishing Company.

The Saturday Evening Post covers, 1921–1922. Courtesy Curtis Publishing Company.

The Saturday Evening Post cover, March 17, 1923. Courtesy Curtis Publishing Company.

The Saturday Evening Post covers, 1922–1924. Courtesy Curtis Publishing Company.

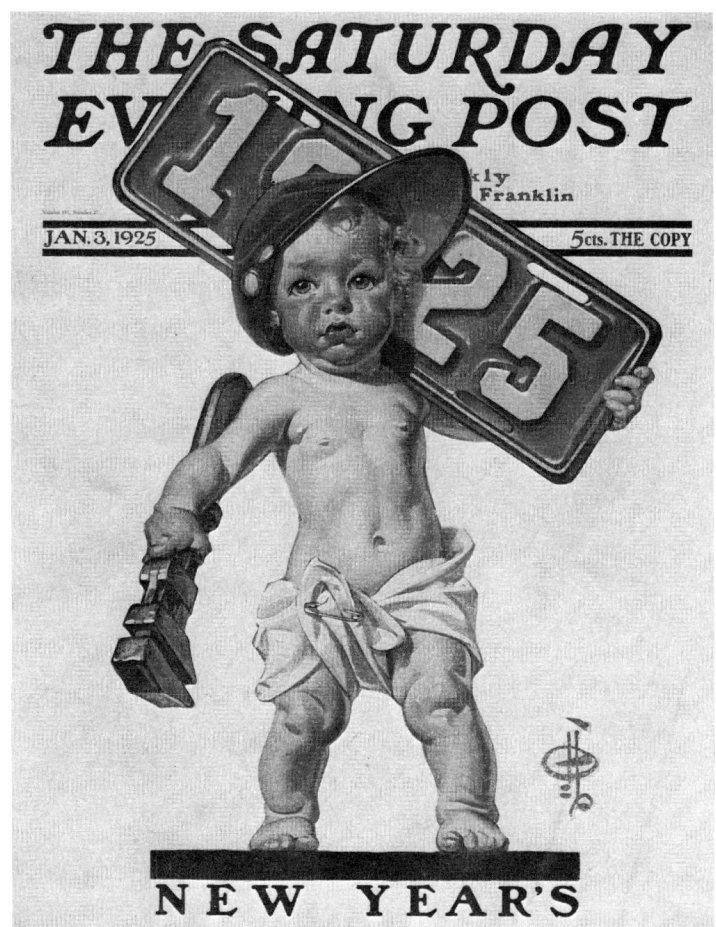

The Saturday Evening Post covers, 1924–1926. Courtesy Curtis Publishing Company.

The Saturday Evening Post covers, 1926–1927. Courtesy Curtis Publishing Company.

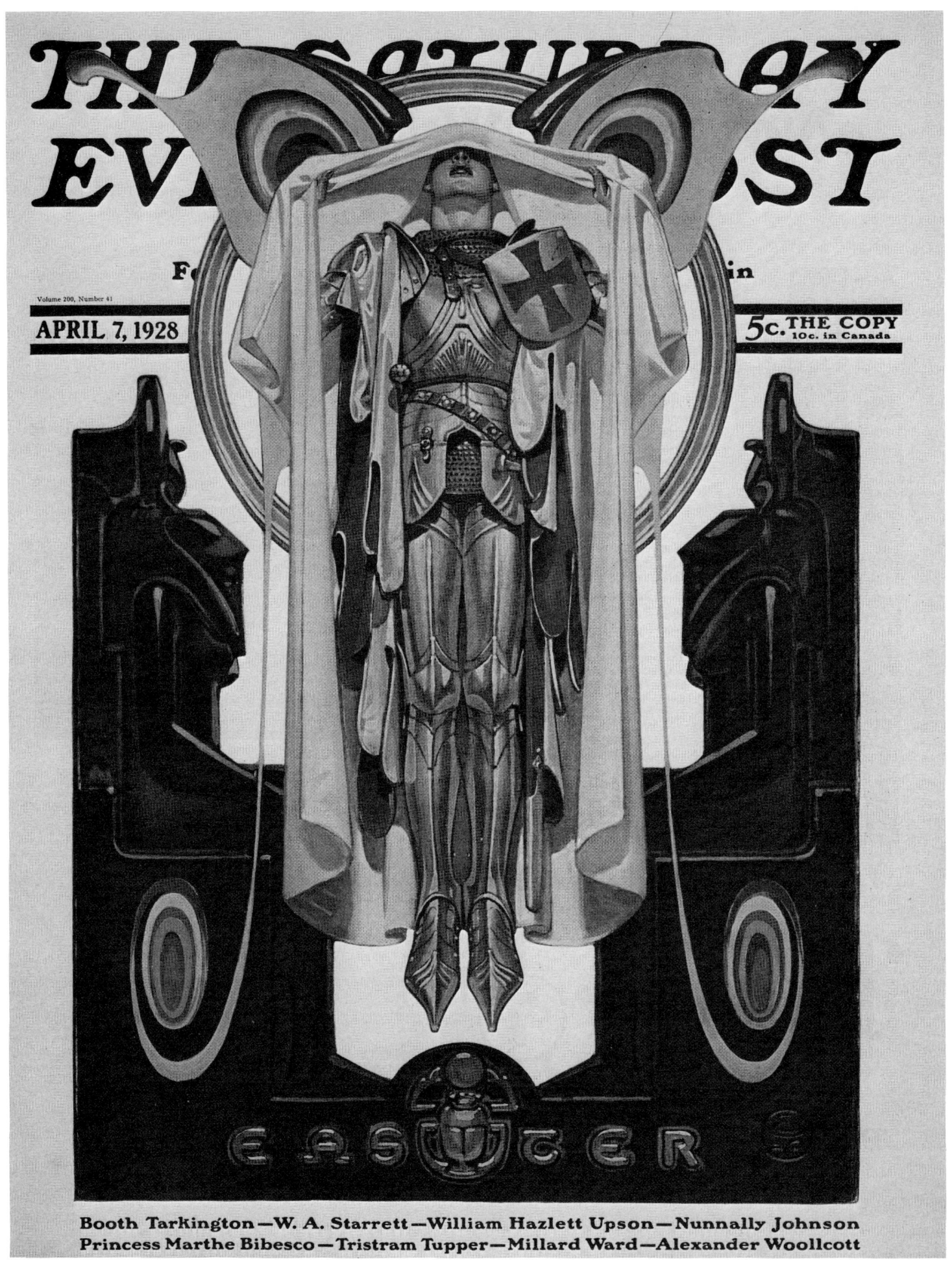

The Saturday Evening Post cover, April 7, 1928. Courtesy Curtis Publishing Company.

The Saturday Evening Post covers, 1928–1931. Courtesy Curtis Publishing Company.

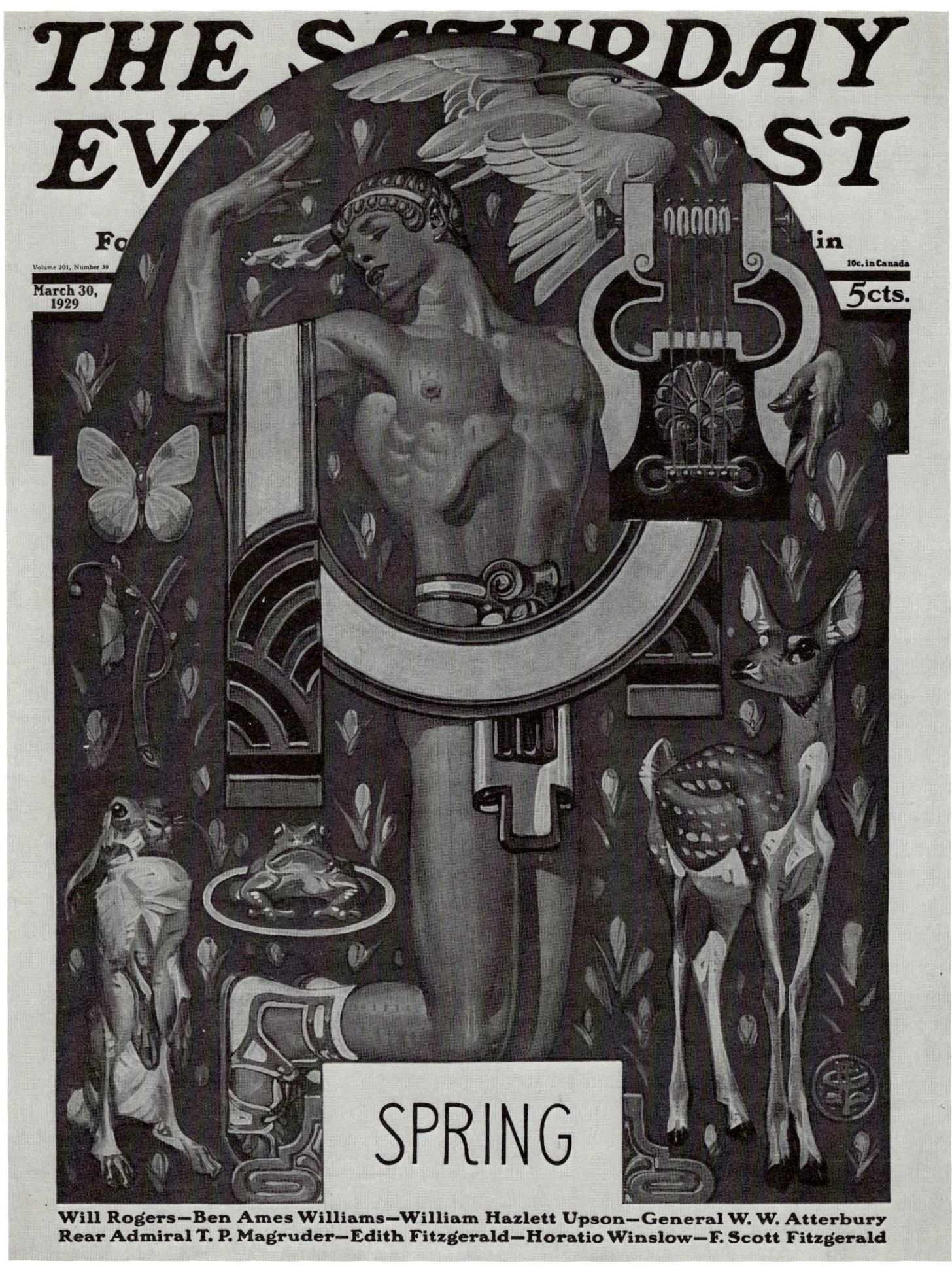

The Saturday Evening Post cover, March 30, 1929. Courtesy Curtis Publishing Company.

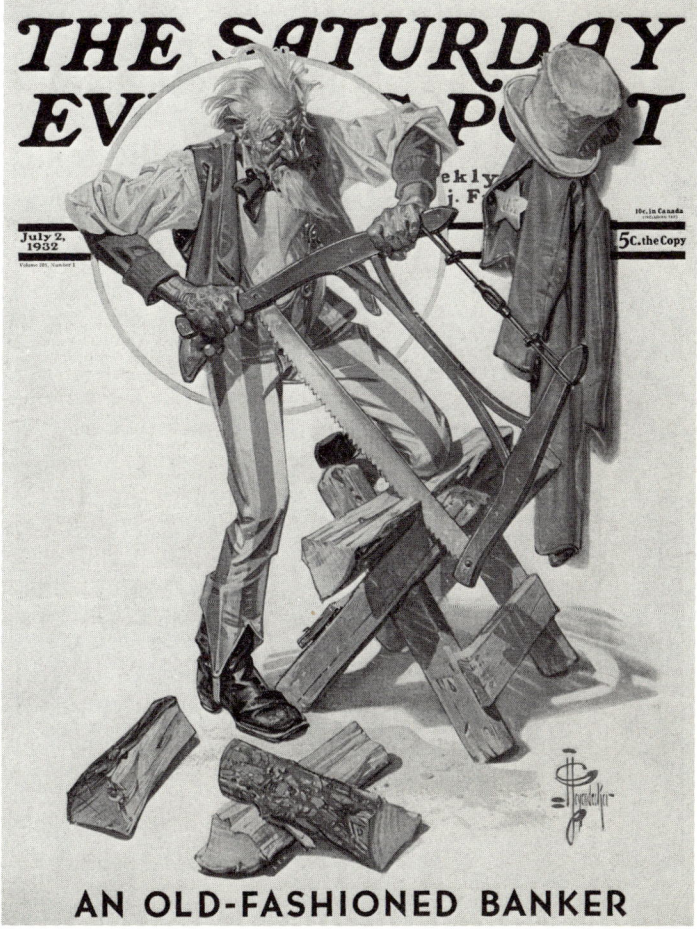

The Saturday Evening Post covers, 1931–1932. Courtesy Curtis Publishing Company.

The Saturday Evening Post covers, 1933–1935. Courtesy Curtis Publishing Company.

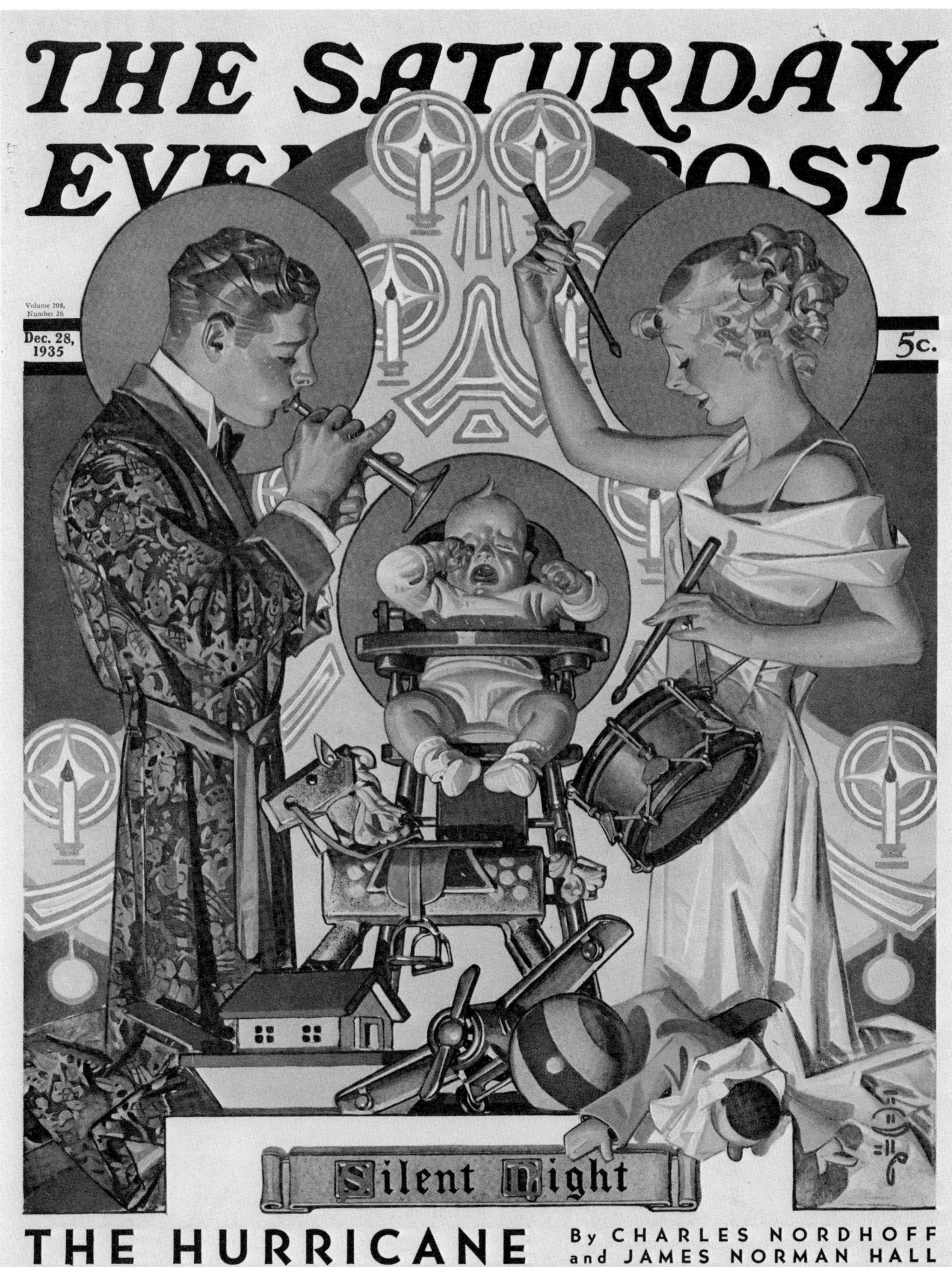

The Saturday Evening Post cover, December 28, 1935. Courtesy Curtis Publishing Company.

Literary Digest cover, December 26, 1936.

The Saturday Evening Post covers, 1936–1937. Courtesy Curtis Publishing Company.

The Saturday Evening Post cover, April 1, 1939. Courtesy Curtis Publishing Company.

The Saturday Evening Post covers, 1938–1943. Courtesy Curtis Publishing Company.

The American Weekly cover, April 21, 1946.

The American Weekly cover, September 1, 1946.

CONCLUSION

It is tempting to try to place J.C. Leyendecker in a particular era of American art. He painted from 1897 to 1951, a span of years which saw the end of the Golden Age of Illustration concurrent with the rise in popularity of many diverse art styles. About 1900, Leyendecker found and established his own style and he never veered from that; the Leyendecker technique was unaltered by adaptation to, or incorporation of, new techniques.

Leyendecker defies classification or identification with trends in art. He was not of the art nouveau era, except in his formative years, and once he left that behind, only an occasional wisp of Mucha-esque smoke reminds us that he ever dabbled. Nor is there a Leyendecker work where interest in the lines and shapes of art deco is evident. There is a minimal parallel in the sharp lines, flatness, and pattery quality of a Leyendecker drawing, but the artist painted abrupt lines with few deep spaces long before *arts décoratifs* defined a style. Art deco and Leyendecker coincidently were elegant and rich, yet they have little else in common.

Why was Leyendecker so popular? Surely because each illustration by the artist set a style all its own—a combination of his talent as a draftsman, his generosity with color, and his elegance. His work can be counted on to be stylistically familiar and yet imaginative in treatment. There is something about a J.C. Leyendecker picture that is recognizable and at the same time startlingly new.

But J.C. Leyendecker's popularity was based on more than technique. His subjects—the handsome men and beguiling ladies—and the human qualities of innocence and warmth, on the one hand, and cleverness and insouciance, on the other, so aptly captured in his work match his painting style for uniqueness and excitement.

INDEX

Page numbers in italic refer to illustrations.

Abbey, E.A., 30
Académie Julian (Paris), 15, 17, 18–21, *21*, 23
Advertisements (plates), *83–126*; Arrow Collars and Shirts, *85*, *88–91*, *100–106*, *108–111*, *124*, *125*; Chesterfield Cigarettes, *122–123*; Interwoven Socks, *118–121*; Ivory Soap, *97*; Kellogg's Corn Flakes, *99*; Kuppenheimer, *85–87*, *94–96*, *107*, *112–117*, *121*, *125*; McAvoy Malt-Marrow, *83*; Overland Automobile, *92–93*; Pierce Arrow, *84*; Rogers & Company Printers, *98*
American Weekly magazine, 45; covers, *160*, *202–203*
"Ancient Irish Sagas, The ("Cuchulain in Battle" and "Queen Meave"), illustrations for, *60–61*
Apprenticeship, 15, 17
Arrow Collar Man, 30, *31*, 38, 43, 81; creator of, 28, 30
Arrow Collars and Shirts advertisements, 28, 30, *31*, 33–34, 36, 81, *85*, *88–91*, *100–106*, *110–111*, *124*, *126*
Art deco, 205
Art nouveau, 18, 205
Arts décoratifs. See Art deco
Autobiographical sketch, 14–15, 17, 24

Beach, Charles, 38–39, 45–46; as Arrow Collar Man, 30, *31*; described by Norman Rockwell, 30; relationship with Leyendecker, 30, 32–33
Beach, Rex, portrait of, *29*
Beaux Arts Building studio. *See* Bryant Park studio
Beethoven, Ludwig van, 20
Benedict, Enella, 15
Bernhardt, Sarah, 18

Bernini, Gianlorenzo, 27
Bible, The, illustrations for, 17, *51*
Bird, Elisha, 23
Birth record, J.C. Leyendecker, 14
Bonnard, Pierre, 19
Boston Public Library, 27
Bouguereau, Adolphe William, 19–20
Boulanger (19-century French painter), 15
Bradley, Will H., 23
Bragdon, Claude, 23
Brandt, Carl, 17
Bryant Park studio (N.Y.), 34, 36, 37, 39

Carson Pirie & Scott department store advertisements, 23
Catherwood, Mary Hartwell, 24
"Centuries Ago," 28
Century magazine (*Century Illustrated Monthly Magazine*), 28; August Midsummer Holiday issue, 17, *66*; cover, *137*; illustrations, *52–53*, *55*, *60–61*; poster contest, 17–18, 23, 127
Chap-Book poster, 23, *68*
Cherêt, Jules, 18
Chesterfield Cigarettes advertisements, *122–123*
Chicago: apprenticeship and studies in, 17–19; early career in, 23–27; emigration to, 14
Chicago Art Institute, 15, 17
Chicago Evening Post cover, *162*
Christie, Howard Chandler, 38
"Christmas Hymn, A." *See* "Great Guest Comes, The"
Cluett, Peabody & Co., Inc., 28, 30
Colarossi (Paris), 20
Colbert, Jean Baptiste, 20

205

"College Football" (magazine cover), *137*
Collier's magazine covers, 28, 33, 127, *133–134, 164–165, 170, 180*
Constant, Benjamin, 15, 17, 20
Crimson Conquest, The (Hudson), illustration for, 57
"Cuchulain in Battle" (illustration). *See* "Ancient Irish Sagas, The"

Davenport, Howard Jr., *26;* as model, 38
Delineator Magazine illustrations, 27–28, *58–59*
Depression, as subject for *Saturday Evening Post* cover, 25, *148*
Dernbach (Germany), 14
Dolly Dialogues (Hawkins), 17
Domett, Alfred, 55
Donlevy, Brian, 28
Duchamp, Marcel, 19

"Eisenhower, General" (poster), *80*
"Enlist Today, U.S. Marines" (poster), *78*

Fitzgerald, F. Scott, 43, 81
Flagg, James Montgomery, 38

Germany, background in, 14
Gibson, Charles Dana, 28, 38
Golden Age of Illustration, 28, 49, 205
Goldhausen, Mathilde, 14
Görg, Anna Maria, 14
Grand Central Station (N.Y.), 38
Grand Isle Casino, 39
Great Gatsby, The (Fitzgerald), 43
"Great Guest Comes, The" ("A Christmas Hymn"), illustrations for, 28, 55
Greenwich Village house (N.Y.), 34

Hamilton, Neil, *26;* and Leyendecker, 36, 38
Hardenburgh, Henry, 18
Hart Schaffner & Marx advertisements, 33, 81
Hawkins, Anthony Hope, 17
Hazenplug, Frank, 23
Held, John Jr., 43
Hibbs, Ben, 45
Hoover, Herbert C. (President), 49
Hudson, Charles B., 57
"Huguenot, The" (illustration), 36, *62*

Illustrations (plates), *51–62;* "Ancient Irish Sagas, The" ("Cuchulain in Battle" and "Queen Meave"), *60–61; Bible, The, 51;* "Christmas Hymn, A," *55; Crimson Conquest, The, 57;* "Huguenot, The," *62;* "Love Songs from the Wagner Operas," *52–53; Ridolfo, the Coming of the Dawn, 56;* "Song of Faith, A," *58–59;* "Victory Unforeseen, A," *54*
Inland Printer magazine: exhibition of covers and posters, 23; magazine covers and posters, 23, 67, 127, *129, 161–162*
Interwoven Socks advertisements, 33, *118–120*
Ivory Soap advertisement, 24–25, *97*

Judge magazine cover, *174*

Kellogg's Corn Flakes advertisement, *99*
Kimball Cafetier, exhibition of *Inland Printer* posters, 23
Kirschbaum, A.B., Clothiers advertisements, 23
Kuppenheimer, B., advertisements, 33, 45, 81, *85–87, 94–96, 107, 112–117, 121*

"Last of the Belles, The" (Fitzgerald), quote from, 81
Laurens, Jean-Paul, 15, 17, 20
Lefebvre, Jules Joseph, 15
Leyendecker, Augusta, 14; and J.C. Leyendecker, 32, 39, 45–46
Leyendecker, Christian Joseph, 14
Leyendecker, Frank Xavier, *12, 21,* 27, 34, 36, 39, *40;* apprenticeship, 17; and Beach, Charles, 30, 32; birth, 14; charcoal drawing of, by J.C. Leyendecker, 21, 22; death, 39; described by Norman Rockwell, 18; dissatisfaction of, with work, 39; early career in Chicago, 23–24; as illustrator, 33, *41;* and Leyendecker, J.C., 18, 23–24, 30, 32, 39; rift with Leyendecker, J.C., 39; studies (at Académie Julian) 18, 20, (at Chicago Art Institute) 17, (at Colarossi) 20
Leyendecker, J.C. (Joseph Christian), *12, 21,* 44; apprenticeship, 15, 17; auction of estate, 46; autobiographical sketch, 14–15, 17, 24; and Beach, Charles, 30, 32–33, 45–46; birth, 14; Bryant Park studio, 34, 36, 38; childhood, 14; creator of Arrow Collar Man, 28, 30; creator of New Year's baby, 25; death, 46; described by Norman Rockwell, 18; desire for privacy, 13, 32, 39; draftsmanship, 15, 19–20, 205; early career in Chicago, 23–27; emigration to Chicago, 14; financial circumstances, 24–25, 43, 45; influence of popular French art on, 18, 23; and Leyendecker, Augusta, 32, 39, 45–46; and Leyendecker, Frank Xavier, 18, 22, 23–24, 30, 32, 39; models for, 36, 38; Mt. Tom Road mansion and gardens, 32, 36, 39, *40, 42,* 44, 45–46; painting technique, 14–15, 20, 33, 205; Pickett

Institute, teacher at, 20, 39; popularity, 13, 25, 27, 33, 43, 81, 127, 205; reputation, 13, 27, 81, 127; and Rockwell, Norman, 30, 32–33; Salon Champs du Mars, one-man exhibition at, 21, 22; studies (at Académie Julian) 17–21, 23, (at Chicago Art Institute) 15, 17, (at Colarossi) 20; style, 14, 17–18, 20, 28, 34, 205; success, 13, 20–21, 27, 33, 39, 127; winner of *Century* magazine poster contest, 17–18, 23; work habits, 24, 34, 36; working methods, 34–35

_____ as illustrator: advertisements, *16*, 17, 23–25, 28, 30, 33–34, 45, 63, 81, *83–126*; books, 17, 24, 28, 49, *51*, *56–57*, *62*; magazine articles, 27–28, 49, *52–55*, *58–61*; magazine covers, 23, 25, 27, 33, 39, 43, 45, 49, 127, *129–203* (see also *Saturday Evening Post* covers); posters, 17–18, 23, 38, 45, 63, *65–80*; sophistication of, 23, 27–28, 43; themes of, 25, 27, 43, 45, 49

Leyendecker, Peter (father), 14
Leyendecker, Peter (grandfather), 14
Life illustrations, 33
Literary Digest magazine cover, *198*
Lorimer, George Horace, 24, 49
"Love Songs from the Wagner Operas," illustrations for, 28, *52–53*

"MacArthur, General" (poster), *79*
McAvoy Brewery, 14; advertisements for, 23, *83*
Magazine covers (plates), *129–203*; *American Weekly*, *160*, *202–203*; *Chicago Evening Post*, *162*; "College Football" for *The Century Illustrated Monthly Magazine*, *137*; *Collier's*, *133–134*, *164–165*, *170*, *180*; *Inland Printer*, *129*, *161–162*; *Judge*, *174*; *Literary Digest*, *198*; *Pittsburgh Dispatch Monthly Magazine*, *174*; *Popular Magazine*, *136*, *174*; *Saturday Evening Post*, *138–159*, *166–169*, *171–173*, *175–197*, *199–201*; *Success*, *130–132*, *135*, *162–163*
Manz, J., & Company: advertisements, *16*, 17, 23; apprenticeship at, 15
March, Frederic, 28
Matisse, Henri, 19
Montabour (Germany), 14
Moore, Frank F., 65
Moulin Rouge (Paris), 18
Mt. Tom Road mansion and gardens, 32, 36, 39, 40, 42, 44, 45–46; description of, 36
Mucha, Alphonse, 18, 19, 205
Mulhall, Jack, 28
My Adventures as an Illustrator (Norman Rockwell autobiography), quotes from, 18, 30, 32–33, 39

Nazi Germany, victory over, as subject for *Saturday Evening Post* cover, 26, *201*
New Rochelle (N.Y.), 30, 32, 36–39, 46; 250th Anniversary Commemorative Booklet illustration. See "Huguenot, The"
New Year's baby, 45; creator of, 25
New York City: career in, 20, 24, 27–28, 36; Public Library, 27

O'Hara, Beatrice, 43
One Fair Daughter (Moore), poster for, *65*
"Order Coal Now" (poster), 38, *76*
Ortseifen, Christian, 14
Ortseifen, Elizabeth, 14
Overland Automobile advertisement, *92–93*

Paine, R.D., 54
Paris: drawing of, by Leyendecker, *19*; studies in, 15, 17–21, 23
Parrish, Maxfield, 18, 38
Phillips, Coles, 39
Pickett Institute, 20, 39
Pierce Arrow advertisement, *84*
Pittsburgh Dispatch Monthly Magazine cover, *174*
Popular Magazine covers, *136*, *174*
Posters (plates), *65–80*; *Century* magazine, *66*; *Chap-Book* magazine, *68*; "Enlist Today, U.S. Marines," *78*; "General Eisenhower," *80*; "General MacArthur," *79*; *Inland Printer* magazine, *67*; *One Fair Daughter* (book), *65*; "Order Coal Now" for U.S. Fuel Administration, *76*; "Rowing" for *Scribner's* magazine, *73*; *Success* magazine, *72*; University of Pennsylvania, *74*; *Up To Date* magazine, *69–71*; U.S. Navy recruitment, *77*; "Weapons for Liberty," *75*
Prendergast, Maurice, 19
Proctor & Gamble, 24–25
Prohibition, as subject for *Saturday Evening Post* cover, 25, *186*
Pyle, Howard, 30

"Queen Meave" (illustration). See "Ancient Irish Sagas, The"

"Radiant Christ, The," 28
Reuterdahl, Lt. Commander Henry, 38
Ridolfo, the Coming of the Dawn (Williams), illustration for, 28, *56*
Rockwell, Norman, 25, 39

_____ autobiography (*My Adventures as an Illustrator*) quoted: description of Charles Beach, 30; description of Leyendecker brothers, 18; on

207

friendship with Leyendecker, 32; on Leyendecker relationship with Charles Beach, 30, 32–33
Rogers & Company Printers advertisement, *98*
Rogers, Will, 49, *201*
Roosevelt, Theodore, 60–61
Roth, Anna, 14
"Rowing" (poster), 73
"Rubaiyat of Omar Khayyam, The," 27

Salon Champs du Mars (Paris), one-man exhibition at, 21
Saturday Evening Post: autobiography of Leyendecker in, 14–15, 17, 24; covers, 25, 26, 27–28, 33–34, 36, 39, 43, 45, 49, 127, *138–159, 166–169, 171–173, 175–197, 199–201*
Scribner's magazine, 28; illustration, *54*; poster, 73
Smith, F. Hopkinson, 18
"Song of Faith, A" ("The Twenty-Third Psalm"), illustrations for, 28, *58–59*
Spanish-American War, 24
Spanish Peggy (Catherwood), 24
Stock Exchange Building studio (Chicago), 23
Stone, Herbert S., Company advertisements, 23
Stone & Kimball advertisements, 23–24
Success magazine: covers, *130–132, 135, 162–163*; poster, 72
"Swarming of the White Bees, The," 28

This Side of Paradise (Fitzgerald), 43
Timken Company, The, posters, 45, *79–80*

Toulouse-Lautrec, Henri de, 18; *Chap-Book* poster by, 23
"Twenty-Third Psalm, The." *See* "Song of Faith, A"

University of Pennsylvania poster, 74
Up To Date magazine posters, *69–71*
U.S. Fuel Administration posters, 38
U.S. Navy Division of Pictorial Publicity posters, 38, 77

Valentino, Rudolph, 30
Vanderpoel, John H., 15, 17
Vanity Fair magazine covers, 33
Vedder, Elihu, 18
"Victory Unforeseen, A," illustration for, *54*

Wall Street Crash, 43
Washington Square (N.Y.), 34
"Weapons for Liberty" (poster), 75
Williams, Earl, 26; as model, 38
Williams, Egerton R. Jr., 28, 56
Wirzenborn (Germany), 14
"Woman with Cat" (poster), 23, *68*
Women's suffrage, as subject for *Saturday Evening Post* cover, 25, *176*
World War I, 30; posters, 38, 63, 75, 77–78
World War II, 45; destruction of Leyendecker Paris drawings in, 20; posters, 45, 63, *79–80*
Wyeth, N.C., 38

Edited by Susan Davis
Designed by James Craig and Robert Fillie
Set in 14 point Fairfield by Gerard Associates/Graphics Art, Inc.
Printed and bound by Rochester Polychrome Press, Inc.